001.94 Chatelain, Maurice.
Cha   Our ancestors came from outer space.
        Trans. by Orest Berlings. Garden City,
        N.Y., Doubleday, 1978.
             209 p. illus.
             Includes bibliography.

        1. Interplanetary voyages. 2. History,
        Ancient. 3. Man, Prehistoric. I. Title.
        0385125356   037184X LC

OUR ANCESTORS
CAME FROM OUTER SPACE

Our Ancestors Came From Outer Space

MAURICE CHATELAIN

TRANSLATED BY OREST BERLINGS

Doubleday & Company, Inc., Garden City, New York
1978

Library of Congress Cataloging in Publication Data

Chatelain, Maurice.
  Our ancestors came from outer space.

  Translation of Nos ancêtres venus du cosmos.
  Bibliography: p. 207.
  1. Interplanetary voyages. 2. History, Ancient.
3. Man, Prehistoric. I. Title.
CB156.C4513   001.9′4
ISBN: 0-385-12535-6
Library of Congress Catalog Card Number 76–50758

Contents

INTRODUCTION

The ApolloSpacecraft

TWELVE YEARS AGO I was living in San Diego, California. I had come there from Casablanca in 1955 with my wife and my three sons at the time when Morocco was becoming independent. After seven marvelous years in Casablanca I had no wish to return to my native France.

One lived well in Morocco, and we had many friends there. Among them a few intimates who worked hard in the daytime and lived it up at night. That was exactly the kind of life that appealed to me. I worked ten hours a day and had five businesses going simultaneously, including a venture in television that really interested me.

We spent seven years in Casablanca, and all went well when suddenly, under pressure from the United States, France decided to pull out of Morocco and grant it independence.

In just a few weeks a well-organized and prosperous country was turned into unimaginable social and economic chaos. Even the most secure businesses went bankrupt because no one paid what was due, and it wasn't even possible to send children to school because they could have been killed in the streets. Disgusted and sorry about being a Frenchman, I thought it better to leave, the sooner the better. But first we had to know where to go.

One of our best friends in Casablanca at that time was an

American of Greek ancestry, who, as the president of the United States Chamber of Commerce in Morocco, had helped me a great deal in the past. He was to be even more helpful now, since he was also the American vice consul in Casablanca.

I went to see him and asked for advice. He said I should have my head examined if I ever dreamed of returning to France, already crowded with refugees from Indochina and North Africa. His advice was to go to the wide, open spaces of California. A mutual friend, now residing in Beverly Hills, would certainly be glad to sponsor me and my family and give the necessary guarantees to the United States immigration authorities.

I was tempted to follow his advice. I spoke English well enough, but my wife, who had for some strange reason studied German as second language in school and had three small boys, was not so easily persuaded.

I finally prevailed, and the very next morning all of us went to the American Consulate to sign the immigration papers and to receive warm recommendations given to our family by my Greek-American friend.

My decision to move to America proved to be right. For the next twenty years I worked for a number of aerospace organizations and industries and was supported by the United States Navy, the United States Air Force, and NASA. I was even reimbursed by the United States Government for the cost of moving my family to the United States, though it took a while to achieve that.

If ever I regretted coming to the States, it was never for professional reasons, because working in California is so much more agreeable than it is in France, where I would never have succeeded as I did here.

After having lived in Beverly Hills for about a month and having found that it wasn't too difficult to find work in the electronic industries, I decided to look for a home in San Diego, where the rents were more reasonable and the landscape reminded me of the Côte d'Azur of southern France.

My first job was a three-year stint as an electronics engineer with Convair Astronautics. Convair was then building the delta-wing F-102 and F-106 fighter planes and the Atlas intercontinental ballistic missile for the military, which were successes, as well as a commercial passenger plane that was not, even after its name had been changed several times.

I started working in telecommunications, which I knew well, and was soon shifted to telemetry, which I knew little about, until finally all my work was with radar, which I didn't know at all. But after three years I had become an expert in each of these fields and was even making a name for myself. I had published some technical articles and had given a lecture. But then Convair's business turned sour. Its commercial airplane still did not sell and the Air Force started cutting contracts, but luckily for me, a competitor of Convair, the Ryan Aeronautical Company, that had built Charles Lindbergh's airplane in 1927, decided to start an electronics division and began luring specialists away from Convair.

So it was that in 1959 I landed at Ryan Electronics as head of the electromagnetic research group, in charge of engineering new radar and telecommunication systems. It was there that I finally had a chance to use my imagination and create new communication systems for which I received eleven patents. That was the great era of electronics, a time that will never come again. Ryan was actually a small company and did not build airplanes or missiles. It specialized in building drones, small pilotless airplanes that were a big success. The Air Force used these drones for fighter-pilot training and shot them down faster than we could build them. At a certain time we even started repairing the least damaged drones, quite contrary to certain principles of American business.

Ryan was also building the world's best radar navigation systems, which gave the most precise readings of aircraft altitude, ground speed, distance covered, and exact aircraft position. One of these flight instruments enabled a military airplane to fly on automatic pilot from San Diego to Washington, D.C., missing its target by less than two hundred yards.

Thus I turned out to be a specialist in electronic navigation. One of my patents—an automatic radar landing system that ignited the retro rockets at a given altitude—was used in Ranger and Surveyor flights to the moon, the latter spacecraft making soft landings without suffering damage.

But even Ryan didn't do well financially. The drones sold like hotcakes but the Air Force needed more than we could supply them, so Ryan lost one contract after another within only a few weeks, something that is typical of the American way of business. As a result Ryan was in financial difficulty. It became clear that I would have to look for another job. Since Convair, the only aerospace company in San Diego besides Ryan, by now faced even greater economic difficulties, I had to go up to Los Angeles to find a suitable position. The job situation was much better there, but I did not want to move nearly a hundred miles north to Los Angeles for several reasons. First of all, Los Angeles is not a city like San Diego. Los Angeles is a chain of industrial suburbs stretched in line over sixty miles and nobody likes to live there if he can help it. Besides, we had just bought a brand new home in San Diego, with a magnificent view of the bay and we had no wish whatever to go and live in the notorious smog of L.A.

So it was decided that my wife and my three sons, together with our huge Newfoundland retriever, Katanga, would stay in San Diego and that I would drive to Los Angeles on Monday and return on Friday, as many of my friends had been doing. It was far from my ideal way of life, but what else could I do?

It so happened that at the precise moment when Ryan and Convair were having their great difficulties in San Diego, North American Aviation was building a new gigantic aerospace plant for 30,000 employees in Downey, a southern suburb of Los Angeles, in the hope that it would receive the Apollo development and construction contract from the United States Government, the space project whose goal was to land a man on the moon.

To start building such vast production facilities before receiving a contract seems foolhardy but very American, because how could you hope to get the contract if you didn't have the factory first to show to the customer? But North American had no doubts that it would get the bid. The company had cemented its relations well with Lyndon Johnson, at that time the Vice President of the United States and in charge of the space program.

At the very time when the new Downey plant was completed, it was announced that North American had submitted the best technical layout for both development and production of the

Apollo spacecraft and therefore had been awarded the contract. It was worth billions of taxpayers' dollars, but nobody complained about it at the time. The only question was who would be first to land on the moon—the Russians or the Americans?

All that was left to be done was to build the Apollo. First it had to be decided how to do it, and no one as yet had a clear idea of what, in reality, this project required. And engineers, thousands of the best engineers available, were needed. To make these engineers want to come and work in a dairy suburb of Los Angeles populated by over a million cows, the pay had to be good. But that was no problem; the money was there.

I was among the very first men who presented themselves to North American, and since I was already known in the industry as a radar and telecommunications specialist, I was immediately offered the task of designing and building the Apollo communication and data-processing system. Nobody specified my duties or functions, because no one at that time knew what these systems would be like. But that, again, was of no importance in view of the rush to land on the moon!

I took my leave of Ryan, and within two weeks I was working at North American on the Apollo project at nearly double my Ryan salary and began to endure the endless commuting of over a hundred miles between San Diego to Downey. Fortunately, there was a magnificent four-lane superhighway almost door to door and it took me only an hour and a half to cover the distance for less than five dollars' worth of gasoline per round trip. At that time I had the best car I ever owned—a pale green Chevrolet convertible with a powerful motor and a white top. For me, who always liked to drive, even from Paris to Casablanca, this drive to work along the seashore was a sheer delight, especially in the fresh air of the early morning, when I had lots of time to think about many things that had nothing to do with the space program.

For the first few months I left San Diego every Monday morning and returned Friday night at suppertime. In Downey I stayed in the Tahitian Village motel, which had been built at the same time as the new plant. The motel was charming, with waterfalls and tropical vegetation, but I did not have much time to appreciate all this. I worked twelve hours a day with little time to eat and sleep. Later, when my work became organized and I put in only eight hours a day like the rest of my colleagues, I would go home to San Diego every day.

When the Apollo project started, there was no communication equipment powerful enough or sensitive enough to make voice transmission possible from earth to moon, not to mention transmission of television pictures over that distance. Such things had to be invented, perfected, and built. Relay stations had to be installed all around the globe in the Tropics with parabolic dish antennas, some over 200 feet in diameter, in such a way that one or two of them would always be in contact with any Apollo spacecraft orbiting around the moon. All these stations had to be in contact with each other and all of them had to report to the Apollo Space Flight Center in Houston, Texas. All the new equipment, built by some twenty different suppliers from all parts of the United States, had to be co-ordinated and made compatible.

How I was put in charge of all this within a few months after I started my new job at North American I will never understand, but that is of no importance now. The only thing that really counts is that everything went well. Everything functioned much better than we thought it would at the beginning, or even better than we ever expected, and I think that it must have happened because of some divine influence, not by human intelligence alone. Since that time I firmly believe in benevolent divine intervention in human affairs.

In April 1963 some technical publications announced the convocation of an international astronautical congress in September in Paris, and specialists were invited to submit subjects for discussion at the conference. I didn't want to pass up such an opportunity and, besides, I badly needed a vacation. Without telling anybody, I sent to Paris the text of a lecture about the communications system of the Apollo spacecraft, by that time very well known to me, and in a few weeks, to my surprise, there was a letter from Paris confirming that my lecture had been accepted and promising to let me know soon the exact day and hour when I was to deliver my presentation at the congress.

That was the exact moment when my troubles began. First, I wasn't supposed to submit any lecture about Apollo on my own.

I should have asked for an authorization to do so from NASA. Secondly, I could not be given a vacation, because I was needed all the time at the Apollo project, not even if this vacation could be squeezed in during the congress in Paris. And thirdly and most seriously, North American unbeknownst to me had already assigned a few other men, with less to do and more backing than I had to go to Paris and talk about Apollo.

But then again, the gods smiled upon me. A miracle happened that I can only describe as benevolent divine intervention. Suddenly somebody found out that during the projected Apollo moon flights, sunspot activity would be at its peak. Sunspots can severely impede and even completely disrupt radio space communication. It should be pointed out here that, considering the number of people involved in Apollo, this discovery certainly could have been made somewhat earlier.

Naturally, once it was discovered, a new countdown schedule —a new sort of horoscope—had to be established without delay, in order to take into account solar radiation from sunspot activity. This activity had to be calculated years in advance of the projected flights to the moon. The missions had to be re-scheduled for the most opportune periods of minimal sunspot interference.

No doubt it was sheer coincidence that at the time the most qualified observatory for sunspot predictions was at Meudon, France, near Paris, where the astronautical congress was to convene. It would have been useless to send an American who could not speak French there to discuss sunspot activity with French astronomers who spoke little English. Somebody was needed who could speak French, had at least some knowledge of astronomy, and knew everything there was to know about space communications.

Believe it or not, of all the people at North American Aviation there was only one person with all these qualifications, and so it was decided that I would spend four weeks in France after all— two in Paris with expenses paid by NASA and two on the Côte d'Azur at my own expense. Remembering the many long faces at North American, I think that that was the day I lost quite a few friends.

That is how one beautiful afternoon in August 1963 I arrived in an Air France Boeing 707 at Orly airport and an hour later was in a Renault convertible, dashing down the Autoroute du Sud on my way to St.-Tropez, without even taking one look back at Paris. There would be time enough for Paris later on. First I had to get to St.-Tropez. Why St.-Tropez? For several reasons, although not all of them shall be discussed here. St.-Tropez is the home of my friend Robert who owns one of the most famous restaurants on the Moorea beach in nearby Pampelone and is my best friend in France. Although I was born in Paris, every time I go to France I feel most at home in St.-Tropez, and that is where I spend most of my vacation time. The Paris that I knew as a young man does not exist any more, and so far I never had enough time to acquaint myself with the new Paris, so I go to St.-Tropez, where I know everything and everybody.

I was back in Paris only two days before the congress of astronautics started when I received a telephone call from somebody I had never heard of and whose name I will not mention here. He informed me that he was greatly interested in space communications and extraterrestrial life and that he would be glad to meet me for dinner to discuss these topics. Since I had nothing else to do that day and since this man intrigued me, I accepted the invitation. It was a fascinating evening. After I had told him just about everything that I knew about Apollo, I learned from him about a lot of things of which I had no knowledge whatsoever, like ancient civilizations that probably had been brought here by astronauts from space many, many thousands of years ago.

My presentation at the congress went very well. I lectured on space communications in general and about the Apollo systems in particular and was swamped with questions not only about the spacecraft communications, which I expected, but also about the possibility of contacting extraterrestrial civilizations and the consequences that these contacts would produce. For that I was not quite prepared.

The congress should have been primarily interested in questions concerning the Apollo spacecraft and the exploration of the moon, but the most lively discussions developed about the possibilities offered by the huge dish antennas of radio telescopes to explore the universe. The Russians were all well versed in these matters because their government supported such exploration, but some American scientists, who knew how badly such scientific endeavors were received in Washington, tried to strike a pose of indifference.

Reminding myself that I was an American, too, I tried to avoid these taboo topics, but I couldn't suppress entirely my curiosity and kept discussing galactic theories with some Russians privately, and a great deal of new information and stimulation to explore intelligence in space came from my Russian colleagues. I cannot give their names here, but without their help I possibly would never have written this book.

As for the Apollo spacecraft itself, I should mention here that, as everybody knows by now, it consisted of three main parts. First there was the command module, a truncated cone about 8 feet high, 13 feet wide at the base, and over 3 feet wide at the top, where the landing parachutes and the radio antenna to be used after the splashdown were snugly stowed away. A tunnel provided passage to the lunar exploration capsule. The service module to the rear of the command module, was nearly 17 feet long and also 13 feet wide and contained all the life-support systems.

Another truncated cone contained the lunar exploration module and its moon vehicle, the lunar jeep, ready for man's first ride on the moon. The jeep was abandoned on the moon, the lunar module left in orbit around the moon, and the service module discarded in orbit around the earth. Only the command module, with the heat shield at its base, could withstand the tremendous temperatures caused by friction during descent through the atmosphere, and the three astronauts and everything that they had taken with them from the moon returned to the earth in it.

Magazines all over the world have described the Apollo spacecraft and all that it contained, but there are still a few interesting things that have not been mentioned. The fuel cells were the source of both electric current and water supply for the Apollo. These ingenious cells, developed for the moon mission, combined liquid hydrogen and oxygen to produce both electric current and water in one operation. It was a simple idea, but somebody had to think of it.

The navigation system was not complicated either. A platform was stabilized by three gyroscopes supporting a sextant and a telescope and was connected to an electric computer in permanent contact with earth. It was enough to turn either the telescope or the sextant and take aim of certain points on the moon's surface or some star—Canopus, for example—and the computer would transmit the exact angles of the sightings with the three axes of the stabilized platform to earth with all the necessary information.

The distance from earth or moon was measured simply by taking the angular reading of the moon's disk or the two sides of the earth. To make these readings, the capsule had to be moved on all three principal axes, and this was achieved by firing small rockets placed all around the service module. To avoid overheating, Apollo had to be rotated constantly so that one side would not be exposed all the time to the sun.

What were the means of communication between Apollo and the earth? At close distances the exact position of Apollo was measured by tracking radar from earth in the C band between 5,715 and 5,815 MHz (megahertz, a unit of frequency). The radar signal was received and amplified by a transponder and retransmitted by Apollo back to earth. The coded messages from Houston to Apollo were transmitted in ultrahigh frequencies (UHF) on the 450-MHz band, in one direction only. Voice and telemetry were carried on very high frequencies (VHF) on the 259- and 296-MHz bands.

When Apollo arrived within proximity of the moon, the communications carriers previously used could not reach that far so all communications went through one single, very powerful, transmitter with a directional antenna in the S band, between 2,106 and 2,287 MHz, with a great number of channels, each transmitting several signals at the same time through multiplexing. For instance, there were seven channels to feed medical information about the physical condition of the astronauts, nine to restransmit the stored telemetry data from the passage behind the moon that could not be beamed directly. The communication systems were improved from one Apollo mission to the next, especially the TV quality.

Today the Apollo program has long been terminated and

nearly forgotten. So maybe it would be useful to recall these eleven sensational missions in the order they were launched. Altogether there were twenty Apollo modules built, of which twelve were supposed to be launched. The rest were to be tested for endurance, heat resistance, buoyancy, and many other qualities.

The first of the dozen modules intended for launch, named Apollo 1 burned up in a flash during a practice countdown on the ground on January 27, 1967, killing all three astronauts on board—Virgil I. Grissom, Edward H. White II, and Roger B. Chaffee. The whole Apollo program was interrupted until the command module could be redesigned and rebuilt so that an electrical fire in the oxygen-laden atmosphere inside the module could not occur again.

Apollo 7 with Walter M. Schirra, Jr., Donn F. Eisele, and R. Walter Cunningham stayed in orbit around the earth for eleven days, October 11–22, 1968, for a breakdown test. All worked well. Apollo was ready to fly to the moon.

Apollo 8, with three astronauts, Frank Borman, James A. Lovell, Jr., and William A. Anders, aboard, made man's first moon orbit, at an altitude of about 60 miles above its surface, the first time the hidden face of the moon had ever been seen by man himself. This first moon mission lasted December 21–27, 1968.

Apollo 9, carrying the lunar module for the first time, with James McDivitt, David R. Scott, and Russell L. Schweickart aboard, hung ten days long in orbit around the earth March 3–13, 1969, to test the separation and rendezvous of the command module and the service module. Schweickart went outside the module and took a spacewalk, attached to the ship by an umbilical cord.

The Apollo 10 mission took place May 18–26, 1969, with Thomas P. Stafford, John W. Young, and Eugene A. Cernan aboard. Young stayed in the command module in orbit around the moon, while Stafford and Cernan descended in the lunar module to less than 10 miles above the surface and then rejoined the command module in orbit.

Apollo 11, with Neil A. Armstrong, Michael Collins, and Edwin E. Aldrin, Jr., aboard, was the first Apollo flight to reach the goal. While Collins flew in orbit around the moon in the command module, Armstrong and Aldrin descended in the lunar module, landing in the Sea of Tranquillity at 4:17 P.M., July 20, 1969, after a flight of 102 hours 45 minutes from the earth. After 6½ hours of rest, Neil Armstrong opened the door of the module and climbed down, the first man ever to walk on the moon. The time was 10:55 P.M. EDT. Aldrin followed him after a few minutes. The Americans were first on the moon! All returned to earth safely on July 24.

Apollo 12 carried Charles Conrad, Jr., Richard F. Gordon, and Alan L. Bean through thunderclouds right at the start, experiencing an electrical discharge of short duration that did not hamper the flight. The mission, lasting ten days, November 14-24, 1969, took Conrad and Bean to the Sea of Storms, right next to Surveyor 3, which had landed there two and a half years before. Some of the more important parts from Surveyor 3 were brought back in remarkably good condition.

Apollo 13, with James A. Lovell, Jr., Fred W. Haise, Jr., and John L. Swigert, Jr., aboard, ran into trouble, seemingly confirming the superstition tied to this number. The mission which took place April 11-17, 1970, was already halfway to the moon when one of the oxygen tanks exploded, knocking out some instruments. The question was no longer how to land on the moon but how to get back to earth as soon as possible. It was decided that the best solution was to continue the flight to the moon, make a loop around it, and come back straight for a splashdown, all the time saving as much oxygen as possible. Everything went as planned, and Apollo 13 returned safely without further complications. The cause of the explosion was never determined, although several official explanations were given.

Apollo 14, with Alan B. Shepard, Jr., Stuart A. Roosa, and Edgar D. Mitchell aboard, went to the moon from January 31–February 9, 1971, landing in the hills of Fra Mauro, using a cart to transport the scientific instruments.

Apollo 15 took David R. Scott, Alfred M. Worden, and James B. Irwin July 26–August 7, 1971, to the Appennine Mountains of the moon. It carried a "lunar rover," an electric vehicle that made it possible for Scott and Irwin to take several trips on the moon's surface, covering nearly 20 miles. This moon "jeep" also made it possible for people on earth to see the takeoff blast of the lunar module on live television, since the rover and its television camera and transmitter were left behind on the moon.

Apollo 16, with Charles M. Duke, Thomas K. Mattingly, and John W. Young aboard, landed in the Descartes highlands. The mission, April 16–27, 1972, brought back the most extraordinary photographs in ultraviolet light of the earth's atmosphere, interplanetary gases, and many stars, constellations, and galaxies.

Apollo 17, with Eugene A. Cernan, Ronald E. Evans, and Harrison H. Schmitt aboard, flew to the moon on December 7 and returned on December 19, 1972. The landing spot was in the Taurus-Litterow Valley. This Apollo mission was the longest both in time and in distance covered and also brought back the biggest load of moon rocks. In addition, Schmitt, a geologist, was the first civilian to visit the moon, all the other astronauts having been military men. With Apollo 17 the program, which had started in the 1960s with so much enthusiasm, ended amid growing indifference and even some hostility from many Americans who were shocked to find out how high the cost of the landing on the moon really was. Some even complained that the live TV coverage of the moon missions had pre-empted their cherished football games.

During these missions several strange things happened. Some still cannot be talked about and some I will mention without revealing my sources of information and with the utmost reserve, because I personally was not there when these incidents allegedly took place. It could be, for example, that both the American and the Russian space programs did bring back discoveries that were not anticipated.

The American space program was an extraordinary success, but it should not be assumed that everything went smoothly all the time. There were many technical difficulties to be dealt with in flight, but with the means aboard, the crews could solve them all in short time. Some breakdowns required consultation with and advice from the controllers and technicians in Mission Control at the Flight Center in Houston.

Difficulties started as early as the first flights of the Gemini program, the second phase in the American push to reach the moon. (The first was the single-man Mercury program.) Gemini

3 blasted off March 23, 1965, with astronauts Virgil Grissom and John Young aboard. It made three orbits around the earth and was supposed to re-enter the atmosphere at a very precise angle in order to achieve the greatest possible slowdown before landing. But the spacecraft's computer guidance did not work properly and it landed nearly 60 miles short of the target area where a U. S. Navy carrier was waiting to pick it up.

Gemini 4 was launched on June 3, 1965, with James A. McDivitt and Edward White aboard, and achieved an eliptical orbit between 100 and 170 miles above earth. With McDivitt photographing him, White went for a "space walk," but when he returned to the craft, the door of the capsule would not close. It took some time to fix that. In all Gemini 4 made sixty-two earth orbits, returning June 7. As on the previous flight, its landing computer malfunctioned and the splashdown was again 60 miles short of the pick-up carrier.

When, on August 21, 1965, Gemini 5 put L. Gordon Cooper, Jr., and Charles Conrad in orbit between 100 and 160 miles up, the heater for the oxygen malfunctioned and then the stabilizing rockets became erratic and other trouble cropped up. Mission Control gave the order to descend, which the craft did on August 29, after a record eight-day flight.

Gemini 6, with Walter Schirra and Thomas P. Stafford aboard, wouldn't lift off the launching pad and the rocket motors had to be stopped—always a very dangerous process. Gemini 7 was supposed to make a rendezvous with Gemini 6-A in space, but Mission Control decided to launch Gemini 7 first.

That launching took place on December 4, 1965, with Frank Borman and James Lovell aboard, and was placed in a circular parking orbit of less than 200 miles altitude, where it waited until December 9, when Gemini 6 finally was able to lift off. Gemini 7's flight set a new endurance record of fourteen days and the planned rendezvous of the two spaceships took place without further complications.

Gemini 8 was launched on March 16, 1966, with Neil Armstrong and David R. Scott aboard, and after only five revolutions around the globe succeeded in catching up with, attaching itself to, and docking with an unmanned 3-ton Agena rocket that was already in orbit. But exactly 28 minutes after the successful docking there was real trouble. For no apparent reason the two linked spacecraft began to spin. The astronauts in Gemini 8 decided to free themselves from the Agena, but the Gemini capsule continued to rotate faster and faster.

The astronauts themselves found the source of the trouble. One of the stabilizing rockets had failed to turn off and was causing the spin. All fifteen remaining stabilizers had to be reignited in turn to counteract the momentum caused by the spinning and to bring Gemini back to normal attitude. When this was finally achieved, only a quarter of the rocket fuel remained. Instead of the planned three-day flight in orbit, the mission had lasted only seven hours when Mission Control ordered Gemini 8 to return to earth immediately.

Gemini 9, with Thomas Stafford and Eugene Cernan aboard, also had to carry out docking with another Agena rocket in orbit 180 miles up, but the Agena wouldn't start as planned on May 17, 1966. Another Agena rocket was launched on June 1, but some trouble on the launching pad delayed the start of Gemini 9 by 100 minutes. Finally, on June 3 Stafford and Cernan lifted off and caught the Agena after only three orbits. However, they could not dock properly because the locking system wasn't fully opened.

On the second day of the Gemini 9 mission Cernan stepped out into space but had to come back in a hurry. He was using up his energy four times faster than had been expected and had difficulties with orientation and finally could not see anything, because his helmet fogged up completely. The planned experiment with an individual rocket propulsion system for the astronauts floating in space had to be abandoned, and the whole mission lasted only three days.

Gemini 10 was launched on July 18, 1966, with John Young and Michael Collins aboard, 101 minutes after an Agena rocket had blasted off in a wrong orbit, again because of a computer error. The astronauts had to use up 60 per cent of their fuel before they caught up with the Agena and docked. The two linked ships then used the big Agena rocket motor to reach an orbit 480 miles up and find the other Agena (of Gemini 8) that was orbiting the globe. The first double rendezvous in space was accomplished.

Gemini 11 took off on September 12, 1966, with Richard Gordon and Charles Conrad aboard, 1 hour 37 minutes after the lift-off of an Agena rocket. It took them only 94 minutes to catch it and dock, an important achievement in fuel economy. The next day Gordon took a walk in space detaching a cable from the Agena and fastening it to Gemini. This operation was scheduled to last for 107 minutes, but Gordon (like Cernan before) had trouble with his respiration, tired fast, and ran out of breath in 38 minutes. He had to return to the Gemini capsule, whereupon both astronauts started up the big Agena motor and lifted themselves to a new altitude record of 850 miles above earth. In this new orbit Gordon made another space walk without difficulties.

Gemini 12, the last of the series, had its lift-off on November 11, 1966, with James Lovell and Edwin Aldrin aboard. It made the link-up with its Agena on the third orbit. Three space walks were planned, but Mission Control discovered some instability in the linked-up pair and refused permission to use the big Agena motor. Instead the astronauts had to climb to a higher orbit using only the small auxiliary motors. That was accomplished and Aldrin had his three walks without incident.

As we see now, not one of the ten Gemini flights was free of hindrances or obstacles, but all missions were accomplished approximately on time and without any loss of life. That was possible mainly because of the composure and the extraordinary technical competence of the astronauts.

The European astronautical engineers should learn a lesson from these experiences of the American space program. They are not, as they think, the only ones with troubles. Three of the most capable American astronauts died when the real drama started, in the fire on the ground in the Apollo 1 capsule during the very last test before the flight.

But the astronauts were not limited to equipment troubles. They saw things during their missions that could not be discussed with anybody outside NASA. It is very difficult to obtain any specific information from NASA, which still exercises a very strict control over any disclosure of these events.

It seems that all Apollo and Gemini flights were followed, both at a distance and sometimes also quite closely, by space vehicles of extraterrestrial origin—flying saucers, or UFOs (unidentified flying objects), if you want to call them by that name. Every time it occurred, the astronauts informed Mission Control, who then ordered absolute silence.

I think that Walter Schirra aboard Mercury 8 was the first of the astronauts to use the code name "Santa Claus" to indicate the presence of flying saucers next to space capsules. However, his announcements were barely noticed by the general public. It was a little different when James Lovell on board the Apollo 8 command module came out from behind the dark side of the moon and said for everybody to hear: "We have been informed that Santa Claus does exist!" Even though this happened on Christmas Day 1968, many people sensed a hidden meaning in those words that were not difficult to decipher.

James McDivitt was apparently the first to photograph an unidentified flying object, on June 4, 1965, when he was over Hawaii aboard Gemini 4. Frank Borman and James Lovell took magnificent photographs of two UFOs following Gemini 7 on December 4, 1965, at a distance of a few hundred yards. The UFOs looked like gigantic mushrooms with their propulsion systems clearly showing a glow on the underside.

The following year, on November 12, 1966, James Lovell and Edwin Aldrin in Gemini 12 also saw two UFOs at slightly over half a mile from the capsule. These were observed for quite some time and photographed repeatedly. The same happened to Frank Borman and James Lovell in Apollo 8 on Christmas Eve 1968, and to Thomas Stafford and John Young aboard Apollo 10 on May 22, 1969. The UFOs showed up both during the orbit around the moon and on the homeward flight of Apollo 10.

Finally, when Apollo 11 made the first moon landing on the Sea of Tranquillity and, only moments before Armstrong stepped down the ladder to set foot on the moon, two UFOs hovered overhead. Edwin Aldrin took several pictures of them. Some of these photographs have been published in the June 1975 issue of *Modern People* magazine. The magazine does not tell where it got them, vaguely hinting at some Japanese source.

There was even some talk that the Apollo 13 mission carried a nuclear device aboard that could be set off to make measurements of the infrastructure of the moon and whose detonations would show on the charts of several recording seismographs placed in different locations. The unexplained explosion of an oxygen tank in the service module of Apollo 13 on its flight to the moon, according to rumors, was caused deliberately by a UFO that was following the capsule to prevent the detonation of the atomic charge that could possibly have destroyed or endangered some moon base established by extraterrestrials. Well, there was a lot of talk and there still is.

It was also said that during their flights our astronauts frequently felt as if some external force were trying to take over their minds. They experienced strange sensations and visions. What seems almost certain is that some of the astronauts did have pychological problems and changes of personality after their missions in space. Some turned deeply religious, some seemed to develop mental trouble—facts that of course could be ascribed to pure coincidence without particular significance.

The experiments in telepathy carried out in space by some astronauts have been discussed and even published. Special symbol cards of geometric figures were used to transmit thought from the participant in orbit around the moon to the correspondent on the surface of the earth. Most of these experiments were successful, much more so than similar telepathic experiments conducted on earth, which generally had a lower score.

Then there is the case of astronaut Gordon Cooper that arouses curiosity for more than one reason. He was the pilot of Mercury 9 in 1963 and of Gemini 5 in 1965, and he was unquestionably one of our most skilled space pilots, yet he never flew an Apollo. Gordon Cooper, now manufacturing skydiving parachutes after having quit the space program, has never told anybody outside NASA what he saw in space. But there are those who think NASA may have removed him from the Apollo flights because he had seen too much.

It is also curious that this man, who is not only an astronaut but also a scientist, has now become a firm believer in extraterrestrial life and civilizations and is convinced that space visitors to earth have been around for a long time, from the most distant past up to this very day. Not long ago Gordon Cooper participated in an archaeological expedition to South America that discovered the remnants of a very old and very advanced civilization dating back more than five thousand years. Pottery, sculptures, and hieroglyphs very similar to Egyptian artifacts of the same period, were discovered, confirming once more the theory that Egyptian and American cultures had a common origin.

It is quite natural for a famous astronaut to be interested in ancient astronauts but one may still wonder whether Cooper did not acquire his sudden interest in extraterrestrial civilizations by seeing for himself in space things that he did not have the right to tell us about.

CHAPTER 1

The Constant of Nineveh

FOR THOUSANDS OF YEARS astrologers and mathematicians have been greatly impressed by the majestic regularity of the stars moving in the skies. For millenniums they tried hard to discover the secrets of this marvelous clock. These skywatchers realized that a very long period of time, one probably encompassing millions of years, had to exist that would represent in even numbers the revolutions of all the celestial objects. At the end of such a constant period, all the bodies of the firmament would again find themselves in their original positions on the band of the zodiac.

These astrologers and mathematicians called this time span the "Great Constant" or the "Great Year," but did not know that indeed this number existed and had been calculated tens of thousands of years before their time to be used by early civilizations but then lost and forgotten as cataclysmic natural disasters and wars destroyed one civilization after another. The astrologers tried in vain to find the Great Constant and finally gave up. But now, by a chain of strange coincidences, this magical number has been found on an old clay tablet from Nineveh.

Around the middle of the nineteenth century there was a French consul, Paul Émile Botta, in Baghdad, in what is now Iraq, who had very little to do. To kill time Botta took long horse-back rides into the desert and the hills surrounding Baghdad. He noticed that some of the mounds had so perfectly rounded forms that they could not have been made by nature. Also, old pottery shards were found on many of these hills indicating that these sites were ancient human habitations.

One day in 1840 Botta gave in to his urge to dig up one of the round mounds to see what was inside. He started excavating the Kuyunjik hill on the Tigris River, just outside of Mosul. Besides the usual broken pottery he found a great number of clay tablets in different sizes, but mostly measuring uniformly 17 by 22 centimeters or, as was discovered later, 12 by 16 Sumerian fingers of 14 millimeters each. These tablets were covered with cuneiform characters, produced with an angled stylus. At that time there was much talk about and interest in this form of writing, but nobody had deciphered it yet.

Cuneiform inscriptions had been discovered for the first time during the fifteenth century in the ruins of Persepolis, in Persia, the ancient capital of King Darius I. In 1472 the ambassador of Venice at the Persian court, Giosophat Barbaro, described these tablets, as did in 1602 Antonio de Gouveia, the ambassador of Portugal, at the same court and the explorer Pietro della Valle, who brought the first samples of cuneiform tablets back to Europe.

Luckily no one at that time could understand these writings, because if the Pope would have read their message and discovered that it was the earth that turned around the sun, or that the biblical version of the Flood was nothing but a pale reflection of the saga of Gilgamesh, or that a great part of Genesis was inspired by Sumerian legends, it is not difficult to imagine what would have happened to the old clay tablets and the people who found or read them.

Consul Botta tired fast from his efforts to collect broken pottery and clay tablets and started to lose interest when he met in Mosul in 1842 a young Englishman by the name of Henry Layard. They became good friends, smoking opium and hashish together, but luckily Layard had to give up on drug smoking because it made him very sick.

Botta told him about his excavations and Layard became very interested. Together they climbed the Kuyunjik hill and Layard was convinced right away that this was a very interesting archaeological site worthy of serious exploration. But Layard had to go to Istanbul on a diplomatic mission, and anyway neither he nor Botta had the means for serious digging. Nothing came of this first project, but that did not discourage Botta. In 1843 he received a grant and started to dig up the Khorsabad hill next to Kuyunjik. He found the first Assyrian palace ever discovered, the castle of King Sargon II, who built this edifice as his summer residence in the vicinity of Nineveh in 709 B.C., after he conquered Babylon. This palace yielded a very rich reward of artifacts, bas-reliefs in huge quantities, statues of winged lions and winged bulls, and more. Most of it landed in the Louvre Museum in Paris, with the exception of a boatload of treasures that sank in the middle of the Tigris when the current tore a large barge from its moorings.

No matter how many fabulous finds were later made by his successors, Botta will be remembered forever as the discoverer of the Assyrian civilization. He also enabled Layard to find Nineveh and the palace of King Assurbanipal, with its tens of thousands of clay tablets. When Botta left Mosul in 1846 he asked the new French consul, an architect by the name of Victor Place, to continue digging for treasures along the Tigris and to send all the loot to the Louvre.

When Layard returned to Mosul he started to lay bare the mound of Nimrud (ancient Calah) where he found a considerable quantity of bas-reliefs and statues, which he shipped to the British Museum in London. But Layard's success at Nimrud hill did not make him forget his primary interest—the site of Kuyunjik, where he hoped to find Nineveh, the ancient capital of Assyria. So he went digging there again. First he sank an 18-foot-deep shaft straight down until he hit a solid layer of brick. From there Layard ordered tunnels dug in several directions. He found a grand hall with a massive portal flanked by two winged bulls. After a month of terracing the Kuyunjik, Layard discovered nine great chambers of the palace of Sennacherib, who reigned from 704 to 681 B.C. and who was one of the most cruel and powerful kings the Assyrians ever had.

Each day brought new finds. Statues, bas-reliefs, whole walls covered by magnificent glazed brick, mosaics of cuneiform signs in dazzling white on turquoise blue. It was here that Layard's crew found the famous alabaster bas-relief of the wounded lioness which is now in the British Museum. But even all these priceless artifacts from the palace of Sennacherib would not have found Layard his proper place in history. What made him really famous was a discovery made later at the same site with the help of his assistant Hormuzd Rassam, a Turkish Assyriologist.

The French and the English were not at that time on very good terms, especially in the Arab lands. To avoid friction, Botta and Layard drew a vague line of demarcation across the Kuyunjik excavation site and each worked on his side. But one day, when his French colleague was not around, Rassam, assisting Layard, decided to start a tunnel from his side straight into French territory. By the greatest of coincidences he hit the library of Assurbanipal, the Assyrian king who had reigned from 669 to 626 B.C. The library contained over thirty thousand cuneiform clay tablets and was a collection of all the science and history known at that time, assembled from all previous civilizations.

In 1846 an Englishman, Henry Rawlinson, had broken the cuneiform alphabet by using a text that was engraved in three different languages on a slab of stone Behistun, in Persia, at the time of Darius I 2,500 years earlier. In Mosul nobody could read the newly discovered clay pages, so the tablets were all sent to the British Museum, where for twenty years they rested in the basement storage rooms.

Rassam had found the tablets in Kuyunjik in 1850. Twenty-two years later, in 1872, a young English Assyriologist, George Smith, began to translate them. Again by chance and sheer luck, he soon found the fantastic tale of the Sumerian hero Gilgamesh, his friend Enkidu, and Utnapishtim, the friend of the gods, who had been warned about the coming deluge, built an ark, escaped the Flood, and landed on the mountain Nizir. Smith had the impression he had read this story before, someplace in the Bible, but with other names. What disturbed him even more was the fact that the cuneiform tablets he was translating were written in 700 B.C. and told stories about events that took place three thousand years before the actual imprinting of the clay tablets. The saga of Gilgamesh and his friends was older than the Bible, so the Hebrews who wrote the Holy Book had taken their inspiration from the Sumerian legend and invented the story of Noah and his Ark, embellishing it with a few minor details.

Unfortunately there was a chapter missing from the story of Gilgamesh. One clay tablet was not to be found in the storerooms of the British Museum. Most likely, it had been pulverized to dust long ago, but Smith had a great urge to go to Nineveh and was trying to persuade everyone that the missing cuneiform page still had to be in the ruins of Kuyunjik. All that had to be done was to find it.

Smith convinced some important people who were curious to read the final chapter of the Gilgamesh saga, and the necessary funds were collected. Smith arrived in Mosul in 1873. It took him only a few days digging at Kuyunjik to find the missing tablet. The benevolent intervention of the gods was demonstrated once more.

Smith continued to search and found about 3,000 more clay tablets at a lower level of the burned-down palace. All were marvelously well preserved, and Smith understood that the heavy wooden floors of the palace, when the conflagration took place, had fired the soft clay like as if it was a kiln, thus keeping it from disintegrating over thousands of years.

His mission splendidly accomplished, Smith returned to London, translated and published the missing chapter of his continuing story of the hero Gilgamesh, and discovered several other interesting stories in the new tablets that he brought home.

One inscription of one hundred fifty-two lines told about the six-year war conducted by Sennacherib—how he won against Hezekiah, the king of Judah, how he destroyed forty-six of his cities and gave the ruins to his allies, the kings of Gaza, Hebron, and Ascalon, and also how King Hezekiah saved his life by paying a ransom of three hundred talents of silver and thirty talents of gold, the equivalent in our present-day weight system of 18,000 pounds of silver and 1,800 pounds of gold. This document is the only one that directly authenticates the same events told by the Bible.

Smith also discovered that King Assurbanipal, known in history only as one of the most cruel tyrants, was in reality a sort of a genius of his time, who had learned and assimilated all the known sciences of that period, mainly astronomy and mathematics.

Assurbanipal did not act as later Christian conquerors did. He did not destroy a single document that fell into his victorious hands. All materials were carefully preserved and brought to Nineveh, where the king's scribes translated and classified them to be deposited in the library. We can say now that Assurbanipal created the first "Encyclopedia Assyriana" and indeed his statue should be standing in halls of higher learning, replacing many of the ignoramuses who, not so long ago, believed that the sun rotates around the earth.

Among the tablets translated by Smith was a certain quantity that contained nothing but numbers, fantastically huge numbers, apparently derived from very complicated calculations. But in 1875 archaeologists did not care for numbers any more than they do today, and so these tablets with the mathematical signs were put aside and forgotten.

I have not been able to find out to this day when and where somebody decided to study these mathematical tablets again, but the translation into our decimal system was finally published a few years ago, and one number stood out. It consisted of fifteen digits: 195,955,200,000,000. That represents nearly 200 million million, more than the distance from the earth to the sun, if somebody would be eccentric enough to measure this astronomical distance in millimeters! Many specialists in different countries tried to find out what this fantastic number could have meant three thousand years ago to the Assyrians, who were not known to be great mathematicians or astronomers. It seemed that Assurbanipal must have found this number somewhere, probably in Egypt, or Chaldea, or even in Persia.

I personally discovered the existence of the number in 1955, when I had just arrived in California. I found it in a recently published book and did not at that moment pay any particular attention. Then in 1963 in Paris, when I was told about the calendar of the Mayas, who also calculated with enormously high numbers, I remembered this number from Nineveh and began suspecting that it somehow could prove there was a tie between the Assyrian and the Mayan civilizations. At that time I made

SUMERIAN MATHEMATICAL SERIES
SHOWING THE NINEVEH CONSTANT IN HOURS, MINUTES, AND SECONDS

60	46,656,000,000
70	54,432,000,000 Hours
	63,504,000,000
	74,088,000,000
3,600	86,436,000,000
4,200	100,842,000,000
4,900	117,649,000,000
216,000	2,799,360,000,000
252,000	3,265,920,000,000 Minutes
294,000	3,810,240,000,000
343,000	4,445,280,000,000
	5,186,160,000,000
	6,050,520,000,000
12,960,000	7,058,940,000,000
15,120,000	8,235,430,000,000
17,640,000	
20,580,000	167,961,600,000,000
24,010,000	195,955,200,000,000 Seconds
	228,614,400,000,000
777,600,000	266,716,800,000,000
907,200,000	311,169,600,000,000
1,058,400,000	363,031,200,000,000
1,234,800,000	423,536,400,000,000
1,440,600,000	494,125,800,000,000
1,680,700,000	576,480,100,000,000

This table shows how the Sumerians discovered the Nineveh Constant by multiplying 70 by 60 until they obtained (in hours, minutes, and seconds) a period of time that was an exact multiple of any astronomical cycle known at that time. But who gave them the exact cycles of Uranus, Neptune, and Pluto, which they could not see, or the cycle of precession of the equinoxes?

some calculations which showed that the Nineveh number could also be expressed as 70 multiplied seven times by 60.

Then one day I remembered that the Sumerians, who were the ancestors of the Babylonians, who in turn were invaded by the Assyrians, used calculations based on multiples of sixty more than three thousand years ago. We still do not know for sure who the Sumerians were and where they came from, but we have found out that they were truly great astronomers who knew the revolution periods of all the planets of the solar system, including Uranus and Neptune. They were the ones who divided the day of 86,400 seconds into 24 hours of 60 minutes with 60 seconds each. Immediately the realization came to me that the number of Nineveh represented the value of a very, very long period of time expressed in seconds! It did not take long to calculate that the number of Nineveh with its fifteen digits was equal to 2,268 million days of 86,400 seconds each.

That was a good start but did not answer the main question— what did this huge time span of more than 6 million years stand for? It was certainly longer than the age of man on earth. Then the thought flashed in my mind that the clever Sumerians were familiar, among other things astronomical, with the precession of the equinoxes—the turning of the terrestrial axis of rotation around the pole of the ecliptic. This movement has a cycle of about 26,000 years or 9.450 million days of 86,400 seconds each.

When I divided the Nineveh number by the cycle of the precession of the equinoxes, also called the Big Year, I had the greatest surprise of my life! The sacred number of Nineveh divided exactly into 240 Big Years of 9.450 million days each. I saw that the fifteen digits on the clay tablet from Nineveh represented for the Sumerians two hundred forty rotations of the seasons around the zodiac expressing time in seconds, not days or years as our astronomers would do today.

Then came my conclusion that this enormous number of Nineveh could very well be the long lost magic number called the "Great Constant of the Solar System," the number that alchemists, astrologers, and astronomers had been looking for for a very long time, while their ancestors were familiar with it more than 3,000 years ago.

Naturally, I had to prove first that I was right, but that did not seem so difficult any more. If the number of Nineveh really was the Great Constant of the solar system, it had to be an exact multiple of any revolution or conjunction period of any planet, comet, or satellite of the solar system. It took some time to do this work and lots of numbers, but, just as I had thought and expected, every period of revolution or conjunction of all the solar system bodies calculated by the Constant of Nineveh corresponded exactly down to several decimal points with the values given in the modern tables of United States astronomers and nearly so with the French tables which give slightly different numbers for the planets Uranus, Neptune, and Pluto.

I have not been able to find even a single period of revolution or conjunction of a solar system planet or satellite that would not be an exact fraction down to the fourth decimal point of the Great Constant of the Solar System. For me that is a sufficient proof that the Nineveh Constant is a true solar constant and has full validity today as it had when it was calculated many thousands of years ago.

However, there is the one case where a slight discrepancy shows up at the sixth decimal place if the Nineveh Constant of 2,268 million days is divided into tropical years. The difference equals twelve millionths of a day per year, so slight that it took me quite a while to discover it, but it does not detract a thing from the full validity of the Nineveh number. Just the opposite— this discrepancy gives us a marvelous opportunity to calculate exactly when the Nineveh constant was created. Modern astronomers and their cesium atomic clocks have told us that because of an infinitesimal slowing down of the earth's rotation, the tropical year is getting shorter by sixteen millionths of a second per year.

This helped me to calculate the true age of the Nineveh Constant and led to the discovery that the Great Solar System Constant accidentally found in the ruins of the royal library of King Assurbanipal had to be given to humanity 64,800 years ago, give or take a few years. Effectively, the discrepancy of 1.0368 seconds divided by the annual decrease of the tropical year of 0.000016 seconds gives us the crucial number of 64,800, the true age of the Nineveh Constant.

In the light of this discovery, the distant past of 27,000 years ago, when Cro-Magnon man painted the caves of Lascaux in

France or the temples of Tiahuanaco were built in Bolivia, not to mention the disappearance of Atlantis a mere twelve thousand years ago, indeed look like recent history. Even the oldest legends telling us about the Egyptian chronology dating back to 49,214 B.C., or the Mayan calendar starting in 18,633 B.C., or the Mahabharata Hindu calendar in 7116 B.C., or the more recent Byzantine or Scandinavian beginnings of time counting in the years 5508 B.C. or 4733 B.C. now seem very believable and most likely true.

One of the recent discoveries allowing us a glimpse of early man was made in the cliffs of Del Mar near San Diego, California. The skull of a *Homo sapiens* or Cro-Magnon man was found and dated by Dr. Rogers, director of science at the Museum of Man in San Diego and Dr. Bada, professor of marine biology at the Scripps Institute of Oceanography, as more than 50,000 years, and maybe even 65,000 years old.

Both scientists agreed that the brain in this skull had been large enough for the highest intelligence and that this individual could have been capable during his lifetime to observe and register astronomical cycles. Possibly he could even have made mathematical calculations as complex as the Constant of Nineveh. But unfortunately we will never know if this man was born on earth or came here as a visitor from another space civilization. Our only certitude is that there were very intelligent men on earth more than 50,000 years ago, a fact that topples all our present scientific theories about the evolution of man.

The discovery that our ancestors of 65,000 years ago knew as much and probably more than we do about the solar system is really baffling. First of all, the birth date of the Nineveh Constant coincides precisely with the sudden arrival on earth of Cro-Magnon man, the first human with a brain volume equal to ours, the first successful result in a program for the improvement of the human race. The primitive man before him had no more than 800 cubic centimeters of brain. The modern man in today's civilized countries averages about 1,600 cubic centimeters. But if people living on earth 65,000 years ago were the primitive Stone Age humans, who, as the anthropologists think, could hardly fashion a flintstone, it is impossible that they could have calculated the Nineveh Constant based on the precession of the equinoxes—a slow westward drift of one degree in seventy-two years, and the revolution periods of the planets, three of which Uranus, Neptune, and Pluto are totally invisible by naked eye.

The only logical conclusion, no matter how much it will make establishment scientists frown, is to assume that astronauts from another solar or galactic civilization visited our ancestors 65,000 years ago and started the sudden evolution of man by improving his intelligence through insemination and mutation and then by initiation into the knowledge of astronomy, mathematics, metallurgy, and other civilized secrets. All this could have happened during the interglacial period between the first and second Würm ice age, when the polar star was Vega and the climate on earth was just about the same as it is right now, if we want to believe the 21,000-year climatic cycle that has been discovered in the geological carboniferous strata. It was an ideal time to create and educate a new superior human race. But how can we prove this?

About fifty years ago, in 1928, European radio operators in France, Germany, Norway, and Holland noticed a strange phenomenon. When they transmitted in all directions a series of signals, they received two series of echoes instead of one. Normal echoes, after circling the earth by bouncing several times on the ionosphere, always came back after a normal delay of one seventh of 1 second.

On the contrary, abnormal echoes always came back after an interval varying from 3 to 15 seconds, as if they had bounced from some object located at a distance from earth of 450,000 to 2,250,000 km, but always a little bit farther than the moon. As usual, this discovery was kept as secret as possible, and, after several years, it was even completely forgotten.

Then a few years ago, a young Scottish astronomer by the name of Duncan Lunan, had a bright idea. He thought that these signals could very well have come from an alien spaceship orbiting the earth at about the same distance as the moon and that the variable intervals between the transmission of signals and reception of echoes might represent an intelligent coded message representing geometric figures or even the map of a constellation, as Bracewell had already suggested in 1968.

By using the usual television technique of so many dots per

line and so many lines per frame, Lunan transferred the various intervals on a chart as he would have done on a television screen. He then successfully obtained several different drawings of the same constellation, with different orientations, but with the same star always at the center.

As Lunan says in his book *Man and the Stars*, as an astronomer it did not take him long to recognize the constellation as that of Boötes and the star as Epsilon Boötis, which our ancestors called Izar and which is located at about 103 light-years, or 975 million million km, from the earth.

One of Lunan's important discoveries was that the configuration of the Boötes constellation shown on his charts was not exactly the same as that we can see today from the earth, and he found an explanation. The big star Alpha Boötis, or Arcturus, is one of the fastest moving stars in our skies. It has an angular motion of 2.29 seconds of arc per year in a southwest direction, and its position in the sky moves by an apparent diameter of the moon in only 800 years.

According to Lunan, Arcturus now appears to us about 7 degrees apart from where it appears on the chart, which means that the map could have been established and transmitted 11,000 years ago. However, Arcturus does not move with a constant apparent velocity, and taking an average of only 2 seconds of arc per year, we obtain a date of 12,600 years ago which corresponds to those of the other stars.

As a consequence, assuming there is an alien spacecraft presently orbiting the earth, it arrived in its present position about 13,000 years ago, and, after observing the configuration of their native constellation of Boötes as they saw it from their orbit around the earth at that time, the astronauts on board have been continuously transmitting signals since then, waiting for human astronomers to become intelligent enough to understand them.

Finally, around 1900, the first radio signals were transmitted from the earth by Marconi, Testa, and others and the Izarian astronauts knew they were now in business. They started retransmitting the earth signals, with various intervals representing a code, and the code represented a map of the constellation of Boötes with the star Izar at the center.

For me, however, the most extraordinary and the most controversial part of the story is not so much the constellation map as the intervals between the different signals from the alien spacecraft. These intervals are always an exact number of seconds of time and, as you know, our second of time is supposed to be a human invention. Up to now, the Sumerians have been credited with the fantastic idea of dividing the solar day in 86,400 equal parts they called seconds.

In other words, these alien astronauts from a distant planet in outer space, who have been orbiting our planet in a spacecraft for 13,000 years, knew from the very beginning that the human race divided the solar day in 86,400 seconds of time. And how could they know it unless they made the division themselves and landed on the earth to teach the humans how to use the second to measure the passing of time?

And then everything becomes clear. Seven and nine have always been sacred numbers. Their product multiplied by 100,000 gives us 6.3 million years. Multiplied then by the 360 days of the year and by the 86,400 seconds of the day, we obtain the mysterious Nineveh number of 195,955,200,000,000 seconds of time. And since we know that the Nineveh Constant corresponds to the exact length of the sidereal and tropical years as they were 64,800 years ago, this seems to indicate that the landing on earth of the alien astronauts from Izar did actually occur about that time or maybe a little bit later.

What happened next, we can only guess. It is quite possible that, after inseminating and educating the human race, they went back to their home planet to report on the results of their mission and returned to our solar system only 13,000 years ago when they thought the human race had become civilized enough. As a strange coincidence, this was the time of the advanced civilization of Atlantis, 1,000 years before its destruction by a cosmic cataclysm, and it could very well be that survivors from Atlantis or their descendants are still in orbit around the earth, visiting us from time to time.

There is however something else in the discovery of Duncan Lunan that seems to have escaped his brilliant mind. As I said before, the ancient human year of 360 days does not make any sense on the earth where it does not correspond to any astronomical phenomenon. But it could mean something for alien astronauts orbiting the earth.

During a terrestrial solar year of 365¼ days, their spacecraft would be sometimes closer and sometimes farther from the sun. We have seen before that a solar year of 360 days would correspond to a distance from the sun 1.009684 times shorter than the present distance of the earth. Assuming for the earth an average distance of 149.60 millions of kilometers and a 360-day orbit for the minimum distance of the Izarian spacecraft, we obtain for that spacecraft a minimum distance from the sun of 148.165 millions of kilometers, and a maximum distance of 151.035 millions of kilometers corresponding to a solar year of 370½ solar days.

This would represent for the Izarian spacecraft an average distance from the earth of 1.435 millions of kilometers for a circular orbit, but it is very likely that the spacecraft transferred from time to time into an elliptical orbit around the earth to get a closer look at the human race or even land and visit them. In that case, its minimum distance from the earth could be as low as 450,000 kilometers which is about the distance of the moon and corresponds to the minimum delay of the echoes.

There seems to be a number of other conclusions that could be derived from the discovery of Duncan Lunan, but I have no room left here to discuss them and they will be the subject of another book. Let us just say for the time being that the discovery of the Izarian spaceship seems to explain the origin of the Constant of Nineveh.

One may ask why the constant of the solar system should have been calculated 64,800 years ago, and the answer may be that it was the time of a special configuration of the planets in our solar system. If my calculations are right, there was at the time a five-fold conjunction of five of the outer planets—Mars, Jupiter, Saturn, Uranus and Neptune—an exact alignment of these planets with the sun which is so rare it takes place only once every 4,627 years. Personally, I like this number "64,800" because it is exactly six times the number 10,800 that was the sacred number of the Chaldean and Hindu astrologers so the number 64,800 must have been the sacred number of cultures long before the Hindus and the Chaldeans.

The number 360 and its different multiples like 10,800; 86,400;

and 432,000 are found in many sacred texts and legends of the distant past. Why did the Mayas, the Sumerians, the Chaldeans, the Babylonians, and the Egyptians use in their calculations enormous periods of time that were all multiples of 360 days or 360 years? Their choice must have had some reason and I can see only two possible explanations. Either the number 360 was given to their ancestors by astronauts or at that time the solar year was exactly 360 days long. The first explanation is very possible, the second one less so—but not totally impossible.

The laws discovered by Johannes Kepler say that for the solar year to be exactly 360 days, the distance of our planet earth from the sun would have to be 1.009684 times shorter than now. That seems to be impossible at first glance, but less so if one remembers the theories of the planet Venus being a planet that wandered into our system at some time in the past and was captured by our sun. Earth certainly had its part in this capture and was possibly pushed further out from its original orbit, giving us a longer year. So it is possible that our year was exactly 360 days long ago and that the Constant of Nineveh represented at that time exactly 6.3 million years of 360 days of 86,400 seconds each. As we will see later, there is another possibility, namely, that of a longer day of 24.35 hours as the result of a stronger pull of the moon which was at some time much closer to our planet. That could also explain why the Constant of Nineveh was calculated in stable seconds instead of days which could vary slowly over the ages.

When after a while one gets used to the idea that all that takes place in the solar system is regulated by one Constant, the mind is ready to start understanding one of the great mysteries of human history, namely, the regular returns of ice ages, that have played a very important part in the existence of the primitive man and in the development of our present civilization.

We are nearly certain now that the periodic invasions of ice from the polar caps are caused by several overlapping astronomical cycles. Some of these cycles are well known while others are objects of heated debates and therefore of particular interest to me.

The first of these cycles is the precession of equinoxes, or the rotation of the axis of our planet around the pole of the ecliptic.

The duration of this cycle is 26,000 years. The second cycle is created by the variation of the eccentricity of earth's orbit around the sun. Its duration is about 104,000 years. The third cycle is the combination of the first two and causes changes of temperature and humidity on our planet. This third cycle is about 21,000 years. The fourth cycle is that of the variable obliquity of our earth's rotational axis in relation to the ecliptic and its duration is about 42,000 years. The fifth cycle, a combination of all previous cyclic changes and possibly one more or even two more unknown factors, is that of the ice ages. This is the cycle that no two scientists explain in the same way. Each geologist has his own theory and refuses all the others.

I am not a geologist and therefore can say what I think. Let me just state that the glacial periods repeat themselves every 126,000 years or so, with a shorter warm period of about 42,000 years in between the two severest periods of ice and then a longer and warmer period of about 84,000 years with a slightly colder period in the middle. It would take five such periods or about 630,000 years for the whole chain of events to be repeated.

This theory is in harmony with the Constant of Nineveh. You have possibly noticed already that all the above cycles are approximate multiples of a common factor—a time span of 5,175 years that I call the "building block" of ice ages. When we divide the constant of 2,268 million days by 1,200 we obtain a construction block of 1,890,000 days or 5,174.648 years. This is very close to 5,175 years and also noticeably close to the Great Cycle of the Mayas that was equal to 5,163 years. So our ice age block is close enough to simplify it to 5,175 years, and if we use it, we obtain results that, except for the Mulberg and Würm glaciations in Bavaria, are very close to the dates given by certain geologists that I do not want to name here.

Of these two, the Mulberg glaciation shows only one glacial period, while the Würm has three. That seems difficult to explain unless the great glaciation cycle of 630,000 years is accepted with alternate very warm and very cold periods every 315,000 years. That would have precluded the first ice age of the Mulberg to take place 350,000 years ago and would have caused the third ice age of the Würm that ended only 20,000 years ago and released the Great Deluge by savage melting.

We can calculate then under these conditions that the peak ice ages occurred the following approximate numbers of years ago:* Günz—599,600 and 558,200; Mindel—475,400 and 434,000; Mulberg—309,800; Riss—227,000 and 185,600; Würm—102,800, 61,400, and 20,000. If this chronology is correct and nothing changes in our solar system, we do not have to worry much at present about the two next ice ages. These should come 21,400 and 62,800 years from now, allowing us plenty of time to prepare and to emigrate to tropical zones if it becomes necessary.

The Constant of Nineveh has many more surprises to offer and I cannot cease to marvel about it. One example is the case of the planet Pluto. Its orbit has an inclination of 17 degrees from the ecliptic as do all the other planets and it was discovered in January 1930 by the American astronomer Clyde Tombaugh because at that time Pluto crossed the ecliptic—an event that will take place again only in the year 2048 when this faraway planet will return to the southern hemisphere. We might add that Pluto is visible only with the most powerful telescopes and its planetary movements can be detected only by successive photographs, all proof that our ancestors could not have known about the existence of this planet. Yet it seems that they did know.

The sidereal year of Pluto has been estimated by American astronomers to be 90,727 solar days. But sometimes, as in the case of the comet Kohoutek in 1975, astronomers too make some mistakes. Since its discovery, Pluto has made only about one fifth of its voyage around the sun so a slight mistake in observations is possible. A negligible error of only seven days in the calculated long year of Pluto would be perfectly excusable. So let's suppose that the true year of Pluto is in reality 90,720 solar days. Now the Constant of Nineveh represents exactly 25,000 revolutions of Pluto and this can be no more a coincidence than the fact that it also represents exactly 240 cycles of precession of the equinoxes. Without doubt our ancestors knew about the existence of Pluto and used its sidereal year together with the Great Year as the base of the Great Constant of the Solar System, the Constant of Nineveh.

We will have to wait till June of 2178, when Pluto will conclude its first revolution around the sun since this planet was dis-

* These names all are rivers in Bavaria with exposed glaciation strata.

covered, to know the precise length of its sidereal year. If it is 90,720 days and not 90,727 as preliminary observations project, we will have more proof concerning the Nineveh Constant. Strangely enough, the number 90,720 is entered on the second line of the fifth group of the Sumerian mathematical series of the constant.

What we still do not know is who the astronauts were who brought knowledge about Pluto to our ancestors. But whoever they were these astronauts also instructed our forefathers about the existence of Proserpine, a planet much larger than our earth at a distance of over 12 billion kilometers from the sun, with a revolution period of 512 terrestrial years.

Nobody on earth can say for sure that they have seen Proserpine and I doubt very much that it ever will be visible from a terrestrial vantage point. Yet our ancestors had knowledge of its existence. Some people might be surprised about my assurance that our ancestors knew the planets Uranus and Neptune as well as the precession of the equinoxes. This assurance is shared today by many authors trying to explain our ancestors' astonishing knowledge of astronomy.

A good example is the planet Uranus which is usually not visible with the naked eye, but sometimes shows up for a few weeks with an apparent diameter bigger than Mars at its greatest distance from earth. Uranus was well known long before its official discovery by Sir William Herschel in 1781, but it took some time to make sure that it was a planet and not a star. The ancient astrologers also could have noticed the acceleration and slowing down of a known planet when it passed another unknown planet. At the last conjunction of Uranus and Saturn on May 4, 1942, the acceleration of Saturn was 2 minutes a day in February, 4 minutes in March, 6 in April, 8 in May, then 7 in June, 6 in July, 4 in August, and 2 in September when the conjunction of these two planets was over. By this same method Neptune was discovered in 1846 by Urbain Leverrier in France and by J. C. Adams in England.

There is some talk at this time about the big conjunction of planets that will take place in 1982. All our nine major planets will be assembled on one side of the sun. Some people have expressed fear that the combined force of attraction could cause tidal waves and earthquakes on our planet. Some even predict that California will break off along the San Andreas fault and fall into the Pacific.

For me, a resident of San Diego, such thought is not very reassuring, but neither does it upset me much, since I have decided to retire to Tahiti anyway. However, for sheer fun, I have made some calculations to see how much influence the combined gravitational forces of the various planets could exert on our earth.

As everybody knows the gravitational force is directly proportional to the product of the masses of the objects and inversely proportional to the square of the distance between them. The planet that exerts the strongest attraction on earth is Venus, but this force is no more than 1/180 of the gravitational pull of the moon. Jupiter has about ¼ the pull of Venus; Mars is about one hundred times weaker, Saturn the same as Mars, and finally Pluto has but one two-millionth part of the gravity that the moon exerts on earth. So we see that no matter how close the planets pull together, no marked influence will be felt here on earth. In comparison with the attraction of our moon and sun, the influence of the planets is negligible. Anyway, we hardly have reason to worry about the great conjunction of the nine planets in 1982 because such conjunctions occur every 179 years and the last one, in 1803, produced neither tidal waves nor earthquakes.

Some might ask why the comets are not included in the tablets of Nineveh. It seems to me that that is not an oversight. There is just so much space on a tablet and the comets had to be left out. The comets that return frequently to our system do not prove the Constant of Nineveh, but calculations on some of these long-distance voyagers show remarkable results. Halley's comet, which will pass through its closest point to the sun in 1986, makes exactly 81,000 orbits in 2,268 million days—a number that should be familiar to you by now—once more it is the Constant of Nineveh.

I could not close this chapter without a word or two about the possible existence of some more planets out beyond Pluto. At this moment there are to the best of my knowledge at least three candidates. First there is the planet which Brady named Proserpine—the same name that our ancestors gave to this body. According to him, the planet is sixty-four times farther away from the sun than we are and needs 512 years for one revolution around the sun. The Constant of Nineveh indicates a revolution period of 187,005 days.

Next is the planet of William Pickering that, according to the Constant, should have a year of 238,536 days corresponding to 653 terrestrial years. Thirdly and lastly there is the planet of Schuette and, as the Constant of Nineveh shows, it should have a sidereal revolution period of 246,951 days or about 676 years. It could very well be that all three of these planets are one and the same—the famous Proserpine that has been seen by three different astronomers on three different occasions in three different positions and at three different distances.

All that, however, does not explain how our ancestors knew about the existence of Proserpine any more than it explains who told them that Mars has two satellites, Jupiter four, Saturn seven, and Uranus two. And how did the Dogons, a primitive tribe of Mali, know that an enormous planet circles around the star Sirius, with a revolution period of fifty years? I certainly do not want to give the impression that I am entirely devoted to extraterrestrial civilizations and UFOs, but in all honesty one has to ask how was it possible for our distant ancestors of the Stone Age to have all this knowledge of astronomy and mathematics? They could not have found it all by themselves. Somebody had to help them, a god or an astronaut.

CHAPTER 2

The Mayan Calendar

THE MYSTERY OF THE Mayan calendar has always been a hotly disputed subject among archaeologists. Everyone had his own theory and defended it firmly. But most of the time this dispute went on between the French and the German archaeologists and that is probably one of the reasons why I became interested. The situation was complicated by the fact that there were two Mayan calendars—one that was quite well known and another one nobody had yet deciphered.

To measure short time spans the Mayas used a cycle of 104 years and this cycle was well known and accepted so that everybody could agree on it. This cycle of 104 years or 37,960 days represented for the Mayan astronomers 1,285 cycles of the moon, 327 cycles of Mercury, 219 cycles of eclipses, 146 sacred years, 104 profane years, 65 cycles of Venus, and 48⅔ cycles of Mars.

The Mayas celebrated in a very original way the meeting of 73 sacred years with 52 profane years. They extinguished all the fires in the household, smashed all the pots and pans in the kitchen, and sat up all night long in fear and trepidation that the end of the world might be there and that they might never see the sun again. When nevertheless the sun rose again in the morning and the Mayas had to acknowledge that the world was still there, they relit their fires and sacrificed a few virgins and prisoners and went back happily to enjoy life for another 52 years. Evidently, every 104 years, when the planets Mercury and Venus had a meeting with the sun, and especially every 312 years, when Mars joined the group, the celebration was even bigger and the number of virgins and prisoners sacrificed was substantially increased.

To compute long periods of time and to make astronomical calculations the Mayas used a calendar that was based on the "Great Cycle"—a period of time that was not precisely known to our scientists. It was vaguely thought that the last cycle had started about 3,000 years before Christ. It was also thought that this cycle had a span of about 5,000 years and therefore had to run out soon. Finally, it was assumed that this long span was divided in cycles a little shorter than 20 years each. For this very scant knowledge we have to thank the bishop of Yucatan, Diego de Landa, who in 1549 ordered all the ancient Mayan documents and manuscripts to be publicly burned because he could not understand these treasures and to him they were the work of Satan.

Anybody who wants to tackle the mystery of the Mayan calendar today has to solve three different problems: the starting date of this calendar, the length of the time span this calendar covered, and the duration of its short cycles. Opinions on all three questions differ widely. Originally, the dates proposed for the start of this long calendar were as much as 520 years apart. Presently this discrepancy has been reduced to 260 years and there are only two groups of American archaeologists who dispute each other. The team led by Herbert Spinden maintains that the long Mayan calendar started in 3373 B.C. The team lead by Edward Thompson thinks it began in 3113 B.C. As the Mayas counted time, this 260 year difference represents thirteen periods of 20 years each that are called "katuns." Twenty katuns, or 400 years, are equal to one "baktun."

The duration of the Mayan long calendar was accepted by the archaeologists with good reason to be 5,200 years, or 260 times 20 years, because the scientists were well aware of the fact that for the Mayas the numbers 13, 26, and 260 were very important. The short cycle, as everybody thought, had to be about 19.75 years, but nobody could explain why it had to be a number that does not correspond to any of the cyclic motions of either the sun, the moon, or any known planet or comet.

When the radiocarbon dating method was introduced, the archaeologists were sure that in no time all the mysteries of the Mayan calendar would be solved. Carbon dating seemed tailor-made for this purpose because all Mayan temples had heavy wooden beams made from a tree called "sapodilla," which has a rich latex content and does not rot. Also insects do not affect this evergreen which is now cultivated to produce chicle, the main ingredient of chewing gum. Furthermore, all inscriptions on Mayan temples mark the exact date according to Mayan calendar when they were built. The Mayas used the vigesimal counting by 20, with a dash and dot system. The numbers were represented by an eye that had the value of zero, a dot that counted for 1, and a dash that counted for 5. As the carbon-dating system was thought to be at that time very reliable, all that supposedly had to be done to bring our calendar and the unknown Mayan calendar into accord was to take a sliver of sapodilla wood from the beam of the temple, find out by its radioactive carbon content how old it was, and then compare its age with the inscribed Mayan date on the lintel of the temple.

In the middle of the tropical jungle of Guatemala stands the magnificent Mayan temple of Tikal built in year indicated thus: one dash, four dots, three dashes, two dashes, one eye, and one more eye—which in our numbers would mean 9 15 10 00 or the Mayan year nine baktuns, fifteen katuns, ten tuns, zero months, zero days, or about 3,900 of our years since the last start of the Mayan long calendar.

The Spinden team estimated this date to be A.D. 481, but the Thompson team insisted that it was the year A.D. 741. Carbon dating was to resolve the dispute and everybody went down to Tikal to obtain fresh samples of the old temple lintel for the laboratory where it was to be tested by the newest, most precise methods of radiocarbon dating.

The first results obtained from burning the Tikal sapodilla slivers indicated that the Spinden group was right, but later tests with a greater number of samples proved finally that the Thompson group was the winner. All were satisfied because each team had won one set of the match, but the mystery of the Mayan cal-

endar was not solved. As we will see later on, the real winner
was the Thompson team that came very close to the right answer
—the year 739 or two years less than 741, as they had projected.

The most amusing aspect was that this astonishingly precise
prediction was obtained from a wrong starting date and a wrong
short cycle. A similar case in history is the precise calculation by
Eratosthenes of Alexandria who 2,200 years ago established the
circumference of our planet by using two wrong values which
cancelled each other and thus yielded the right answer.

I had long been intrigued by the mysteries of the Mayan calendar but never had the time to take a closer look. Then, after a
dinner date in Paris with a French specialist in Mayan culture, I
decided to try the impossible. I knew that the Mayas, like the
Sumerians, were great astronomers and I had long suspected the
two cultures had something in common. The Mayas also knew of
the precession of the equinoxes and the existence of Uranus and
Neptune. They had calculated the periods of revolution and the
conjunctions of different planets and discovered, as I already
mentioned, the equivalent astronomical cycles—such as 65 revolutions of Venus which are equal to 104 solar years, or 327 revolutions, of Mercury. They also used the cycle of 33,968 days to
predict eclipses, and this cycle was equal to 5 lunar precessions,
93 solar years, 196 eclipses, and 1,150 lunar months. We will look
at these figures later once more. Meanwhile, the Mayas had also
discovered a cycle of 1,886,040 days that represented exactly 260
conjunctions of Jupiter and Saturn, 2,310 of Mars and Jupiter,
2,418 of earth and Mars, and 3,230 of earth and Venus.

This particular cycle was the key to the mystery of the Mayan
calendar. It was based on the conjunctions of Jupiter and Saturn,
something nobody had cared to consider. All other periods of
sidereal or synodic revolution of all planets had been tried, but
somehow nobody had tested the conjunctions between the
planets.

The conjunction period of Jupiter and Saturn is in reality
7,253.445 days, but the rounded-out Mayan value of 7,254 days is
valid because they did not use decimal parts and counted in
whole days only. So the Great Cycle of the 260 Mayan conjunctions was 1,886,040 days, or 5,163.8 of our years.

I finally discovered that all Mayan chronology was based on

MAYAN ASTRONOMICAL CALENDAR
FROM 3144 B.C. TO 2020 A.D.

MAYAN GRAND CYCLE OF 260 KATUNS OR 5163 YEARS

Baktuns

	0	1	2	3	4	5	6	7	8	9	10	11	12
0	3144	2747	2350	1953	1555	1158	0761	0364	0034	0431	0828	1226	1623
1	3124	2727	2330	1933	1536	1138	0741	0344	0054	0451	0848	1245	1643
2	3104	2707	2310	1913	1516	1119	0721	0324	0074	0471	0868	1265	1662
3	3084	2687	2290	1893	1496	1099	0702	0304	0094	0491	0888	1285	1682
4	3065	2667	2270	1873	1476	1079	0682	0285	0114	0511	0908	1305	1702
5	3045	2648	2250	1853	1456	1059	0662	0265	0133	0531	0928	1325	1722
6	3025	2628	2231	1833	1436	1039	0642	0245	0153	0550	0948	1345	1742
7	3005	2608	2211	1814	1416	1019	0622	0225	0173	0570	0967	1365	1762
8	2985	2588	2191	1794	1397	0999	0602	0205	0193	0590	0987	1384	1782
9	2965	2568	2171	1774	1377	0980	0582	0185	0213	0610	1007	1404	1801
10	2945	2548	2151	1754	1357	0960	0563	0165	0233	0630	1027	1424	1821
11	2926	2528	2131	1734	1337	0940	0543	0146	0253	0650	1047	1444	1841
12	2906	2509	2111	1714	1317	0920	0523	0126	0272	0670	1067	1464	1861
13	2886	2489	2092	1694	1297	0900	0503	0106	0292	0689	1087	1484	1881
14	2866	2469	2072	1675	1277	0880	0483	0086	0312	0709	1106	1504	1901
15	2846	2449	2052	1655	1258	0860	0463	0066	0332	0729	1126	1523	1921
16	2826	2429	2032	1635	1238	0841	0443	0046	0352	0749	1146	1543	1940
17	2806	2409	2012	1615	1218	0821	0424	0026	0372	0769	1166	1563	1960
18	2787	2389	1992	1595	1198	0801	0404	0007	0392	0789	1186	1583	1980
19	2767	2370	1972	1575	1178	0781	0384	0014	0411	0809	1206	1603	2000
20	2747	2350	1953	1555	1158	0761	0364	0034	0431	0828	1226	1623	2020

Katuns

This Mayan calendar of 1,886,040 days was based on 260 conjunctions of Jupiter and Saturn, which occur every 7,254 days. It was divided into 13 baktuns of 20 katuns each, as well as into 7,254 sacred years of 260 days or 5,239 calendar years of 360 days. Each baktun also represented 186 synodic revolutions of Mars or 5,310 sidereal revolutions of the Moon.

several Great Cycles of 5,163 years, or 260 conjunctions, each, counted in succession, and once the duration and the rhythm of the Great Cycle was established, it was not difficult to find the starting point of the Mayan calendar. I presumed that at the start of the last Great Cycle some remarkable astronomic phenomenon must have occurred. The joint arrival of four planets in the same corner of the sky, the meeting of Jupiter, Saturn, Uranus, and Neptune takes place every 4,627 years after each of the planets has finished an exact number of conjunctions and is again lined up with the others. And the last time such a phenomenon took place was the year 1484 of the Christian era.

Stepping now 4,627 years back I marked the year 3144 B.C. and took three more times the same amount of time passed to arrive at the date 18,633 B.C., a date only three years off the year 18,630 B.C. mentioned as an important date in a sacred Mayan codex preserved in the Vatican. For me that constitutes proof. And also, if my calculations are reasonably accurate, some other quite rare astronomical occurrence took place in the skies over the Mayan temples in that year—a double eclipse of the sun and of the moon during the same year. The exact dates were November 23 for the eclipse of the sun and June 3 for the moon.

When I also discovered that the count of days in each sacred year was 260, the same number as katuns in the Great Cycle, all the pieces of the jigsaw puzzle began to fall into place. For the Mayas the katun of 7,254 days was not only a measure of time but also an astronomical unit to express the synodic periods of revolution of planets, or the count of days needed for each planet to be realigned with the sun and the earth. For example, 5 katuns were equal to 313 revolutions of Mercury, 13 katuns were equal to 121 revolutions of Mars, or 27 katuns were equal to 7 returns of Halley's comet.

It seems that, like the Sumerians, the Mayas were familiar with the Constant of Nineveh—but in another form. Their time was counted in days, not seconds. For years the professional archaeologists searching the ruins of the Mayan temples had found fantastically high numbers engraved in stone. These numbers correspond to millions of years and billions of days, while the officially recognized age of mankind, according to scientists of that day, was only 6,000 years—one reason why the gigantic numbers meant nothing to those early archaeologists and were simply dismissed. Many years later a courageous author sug-

MAYAN ASTRONOMICAL CLOCK

CLASSICAL PERIOD FROM 233 TO 1027 AD

THE OUTER CIRCLE INDICATES THE DATES OF OUR PRESENT CALENDAR
THE MIDDLE CIRCLE INDICATES THE MAYAN DATES IN BAKTUNS AND KATUNS
THE INNER CIRCLE INDICATES THE MAYAN DATES IN TUNS

This clock showing the classical Mayan period, A.D. 233–1027, is based on the same principle as the calendar, but for only 290,160 days, or 372 Mars cycles. The Mayas also had a shorter calendar of 37,960 days representing 65 Venus cycles of 584 days, or 104 solar years of 365 days, or 146 sacred years of 260 days. From the center, circles indicate Mayan years, Mayan baktuns and katuns, and corresponding years of our present calendar.

The date of this Mayan disk had been estimated as A.D. 587 but it could be much older. It actually shows, since the origin of the calendar, an elapsed time of 11 days, 14 months, 12 years, 17 katuns, 7 baktuns, and 9 Grand Cycles. That seems to indicate the year 14 B.C. for the disk and the year 49,611 B.C. for the origin of the Mayan calendar (estimated by others as 18,633 B.C.). After all, it is only 1 baktun before the start of the Egyptian calendar in 49,214 B.C.

gested that one of these mysterious numbers represented a cycle of 23,040 millions of days, or 64 millions of Mayan years of 360 days each, called an "alautun." But still nobody paid any attention, and the huge Mayan numbers were forgotten once more.

I must admit myself that when I first heard about the gigantic Mayan numbers I saw no importance in them and simply decided the ancient Mayas had been addicted to big numbers as some people are addicted to drugs, religion, or sex. It was only after I had discovered the Constant of Nineveh and the secret of the Mayan calendar that my new respect for the achievements of our ancestors made me ask if there could be some common knowledge between the Sumerians who counted by sixty and the Mayas who counted by twenty, while most other people of antiquity used the decimal system like the Egyptians or counted by the dozen like the ancient Gauls or Babylonians.

One day as I looked at some notes taken years ago in Paris during a long discussion with my French specialist in Mayan culture, I noticed two especially mysterious numbers that had been found engraved in some Mayan ruins. One was 34,020 millons of days or about 93 millions of years and the other 147,420 millions of days or a little more than 403 millions of years. Expressed in sacred years of 260 days, the second number represented exactly 567 million years.

It is difficult to blame the archaeologists for ignoring these numbers. But since I am not an archaeologist and am used to the huge numbers involved in space exploration, the Mayan numbers did not discourage me, and before long I saw that the 34,020 million days represented fifteen times the Constant of Nineveh, while 147,420 million days represented it sixty-five times.

I spent a lot of time pondering why the Mayas would have used these huge constants before the answer came to me: They made all their calculations by 26 or 260 conjunctions. So they needed a constant of the solar system that would be divisible by 260, and since the Nineveh Constant represented for them 312,680 conjunctions, which cannot be divided by either 26 or 260, they invented a new constant of 34,020 millions of days that represented 180,392 small cycles of 26 conjunctions and another one of 147,420 millions of days that represented 78,170 great cycles of 260 conjunctions.

It is surely beyond imagination to think that thousands of years ago the Mayas could have, all by themselves, calculated a constant of 147,420 millions of days—a number that has twelve digits. But it is even more surprising to see that the same number, only sixty-five times smaller and expressed in seconds instead of days, has been used by Sumerians, a nation on the opposite side of the globe. This fact seems to indicate that the Mayas and the Sumerians must have had direct connections with each other or that they shared a common origin.

I would like to emphasize here that the first constant which the Mayas used equals exactly 3,600 Sumerian cycles of precession of the equinoxes of 9,450,000 days each. The reader can draw his own conclusions. But the number 3,600 certainly seems to be the root of all the astronomical calculations our ancestors made, as it is a basic number in the geometry of our planet. We have exactly 3,600 tenths of one degree in the circumference of the globe and at the equator each of these parts is equal to 36,000 Babylonian feet.

Most of the calendars of antiquity, no matter where, have been calculated from the movements of the celestial bodies and the Mayan calendar is certainly not the only one that has been worked out from the conjunctions of Jupiter and Saturn. It is certainly interesting to observe how many important religious and political events coincide with the alignments of these two planets.

The conjunctions of Jupiter and Saturn behind the sun take place quite rarely. The last such event happened in 1881 and the one before that in 503 B.C. Yet this cycle of 2,383 years was known to the astrologers many thousands of years before our era, as it repeated itself in the years 10,035; 7,652; 5,269; and 2,886 before Christ. The oldest date comes close to the time when the fabled Atlantis disappeared and the second oldest seems to indicate the time of the Great Flood described in the Bible.

Among other ancient calendars, some were based on relative motions of the moon and sun and the most frequently used cycle was 10,800 years, common to the Hindus, the Sumerians, and the Babylonians. Forty of these cycles made the great cycle of the Hindus and the great year of Berossus, high priest of Babylon.

The figure 10,800 also repeats itself in many other places. Multiples or fractions of this number can be found in sacred texts from all around the world. The Rig-Veda, the most important sacred book of the Hindus, has 10,800 verses and the altar of the

Vedic god Agni has been built of exactly 10,800 bricks. The Greek philosopher Heraclitus, who 2,500 years ago was the first to propose that matter is transformable, counted time in eons of 10,800 years each. Another example of this number is to be found in Cambodia in the temple of Angkor Wat. This place is much older than most people think and it is decorated with 540 statues along five avenues. Each statue represents 20 years of time. They are erected exactly like the stone pillars, or steles of the Mayas which also represent 20 years each, and when you add them all, they represent 10,800 years. Finally, the German legend of the Nibelungs speaks of the 10,800 souls of dead warriors who enter the gates of Walhalla—the abode of the immortal heroes.

Can one really believe that all this is a coincidence or must one assume that all the legends containing the same exact number could have a common source of origin, be it terrestrial, solar, or galactic? These enormous 10,800- or 432,000-year spans prove at least that our ancestors many thousands of years ago had no fear of complicated calculations and that indeed they knew how to predict eclipses and other astronomical events for thousands of years in advance of their own time. But who were the gods or the astronauts who taught them this wisdom and presumably also brought them agriculture, metallurgy, and many other skills leading to civilization?

The answer may well be buried in the ancient Mayan city of Palenque in southern Mexico. It was there that on June 15, 1952, Alberto Ruiz, a Mexican archaeologist, made a fantastic archaeological discovery. A few years earlier Ruiz had started to clear the ruins in Palenque and found a stairway leading to the inside of a step pyramid. The passage was clogged by debris. It took several years to clear the stairs and break through several walls. All the work in Palenque had to be done during a few short months in between the rainy seasons. But when it was done and Ruiz went down into the stairwell, he found a magnificent burial chamber and an enormous bas-relief tombstone. The stone slab was 1,600 mm wide, 2,200 mm high, and 250 mm thick. It weighed over 2 tons. And not one of these dimensions fitted the measurement systems of the Mayas or other Amerindian civilizations. Neither the Maya foot measuring 300 mm nor the

Tiahuanaco foot of 297 mm, nor the Cuenca (Ecuador) foot of 348 mm seemed applicable to measure the Palenque tomb cover. It was clear that the builders of this tomb had used some much older system of measurement, possibly an ancestor of the metric system.

To top it all, the very well-preserved bas-relief depicted an astronaut sitting at the controls of a space vehicle! And it was unmistakably a spacecraft propelled by a jet exhaust. As a consequence, it is not difficult to imagine the amazement and even the furor of most establishment archaeologists when they heard of this discovery. And as is usual with them, crying "Fraud!" was their only explanation.

However, the grave itself contained more shocks. When the heavy tombstone was finally lifted, the sarcophagus contained the well-preserved skeleton of a white man who must have been at least 180 cm, or 70 inches tall; but the average height of a Maya rarely exceeded 150 cm, or 60 inches. The bas-relief was engraved with twenty-four hieroglyphs not yet deciphered. The sarcophagus was in the form of a fish—a symbol common to many ancient religions and probably hinting at the aquatic origin of man. Did Ruiz discover the tomb of the great Mayan god Kukulcan who, according to the legend, was tall and blond with a beard and blue eyes and had arrived one day from the land where the sun rises?

CHAPTER 3

The Secret of the Pyramid

SO MANY BOOKS HAVE been written about the Great Pyramid of Cheops at Giza that it seems impossible today to write anything new about the subject. This statement is not quite true, however, since there is always some previously overlooked angle that can bring out new facts.

The majority of men specializing in exploring and mapping of the Great Pyramid agree today that the length of its base was 440 Egyptian cubits, one such cubit being one and a half millionth part of the territorial length of Egypt. That makes the Egyptian cubit equal to 0.524148 meters and gives the pyramid a base length of 230.625 meters. This is slightly different from certain measurements made in inches, but the value of an inch in antiquity is not clearly defined and nobody can really say how long the base of the pyramid was because its entire outer layer has been removed and used to build the mosques and palaces of Cairo. Also more than one earth tremor has shaken the pyramid during its 5,000 years of existence, one of the most severe being an earthquake whose epicenter was the Aegean island of Thera, which is thought by some to have destroyed the Cretan civilization in 1521 B.C.

The main point of disagreement about the Great Pyramid of Cheops is its height. It can not be measured today any more because the whole top part has been carried away and destroyed

by men and nature. Its height must have measured between 279
and 281 cubits, but it is very difficult to compute because three
different mathematical concepts were used in building the pyramid and all three of these ways of calculating are slightly at odds
with the methods of modern mathematicians working with decimals.

The first concept calls for exact proportions between the pyramid and our planet earth. The height of the pyramid should be
proportional to the radius of the earth and the perimeter should
be proportional to the circumference. The second principle
requires that each face of the sides should be equal to the square
of the height. The third demands that the volume of the pyramid be of exactly 18 millions of cubic cubits.

At first glance these three conditions seem irreconcilable. But
let us try nevertheless to reconcile them. To do this, we will have
to calculate the triangle formed by a half base line, one side of
the pyramid, and the apothem—the shortest line between the
summit of the pyramid and the middle point of one base line.
We will have to make all calculations in cubits, and to make us
understand the feeling the Egyptian architect must have had
5,000 years ago we must remember all the time that the proportion between the height and half base of the pyramid has to be a
very simple one because hundreds of thousands of stones will
have to be cut to these specifications.

The first condition calls for the proportion between the height
and the half base to be 1.273239, or 4 divided by 3.141592 (π).
In that case, with a half base of 220, the height is equal to
280.112 cubits and the apothem 356.178, which gives us the volume of the pyramid as 18,076,605 cubic cubits. Conditions two
and three are not fulfilled but the dimensions are proportional to
those of our earth—the height to the radius and the perimeter to
the circumference.

The second condition exacts a proportion of 1.272019, the
square root of 1.618034 which is the Golden Section or factor ϕ.
Then the height is 279.844 cubits, the apothem 355.967 cubits,
and the volume 18,059,288 cubic cubits. Conditions one and
three are not reached but the surface of one face is equal to the
square of the height.

Condition three requires the proportion between the height

and the half base to be 1.267843. In such case, the height is equal to 278.925 cubits and the apothem to 355.245. The volume now is exactly 18 million cubic cubits, but conditions one and two are not satisfied. As one can see from these examples, the three conditions are incompatible with modern mathematics using the decimal system. But the Egyptians did not use such a system; instead of decimal parts they used fractions. And if we use fractions, these problems disappear.

For the Egyptians, as for all ancient mathematicians, the factor π was 22 divided by 7, or the fraction—22/7 in decimal expression 3.14857. The factor ϕ was the fraction 196/121, or 1.619834. If expressed as simple fractions both factors are related because the square root of factor ϕ is now equal to 4 divided by factor π, or 1.272727. Here you have the secret of the Great Pyramid, or at least one of its secrets.

With this factor, 1.272727, and a half base of 220, the height is exactly 280 cubits and the apothem 356.089. The volume is 18,069,333 cubic cubits. The first two conditions are fulfilled in Egyptian fractions but the third is not. To satisfy it we will have to discover another secret of the Great Pyramid—that its base, contrary to previous assumptions, is not exactly a square.

One of the strange qualities of the Great Pyramid is the fact that its faces are not entirely flat. They are concave and the apothem recedes by about one cubit. The first to discover this concavity was Edme François Jomard, one of the French scientists accompanying Napoleon on his Egyptian expedition in 1798. A sketch of the Great Pyramid done by Napoleon himself is still extant and it clearly shows the receding apothem on the two visible faces. This anomaly was forgotten for nearly a century until, in 1881, Sir Flinders Petrie rediscovered it and measured it to be 37 inches, or 1.8 cubits, on the north face. This value was too big, but what can you expect from ancient measurements? Besides, there is now an excellent modern aerial photograph showing the dihedral angle of the sides in superb clarity.

As could be expected, each pyramidologist has his own explanation for this angle. Fact is that it renders the outlines more distinct and the shadows more recognizable, which was of great importance for the astronomers because it made their observations much more precise. Also the luminosity of the faces is enhanced

PYRAMID OF CHEOPS

Original Dimensions in Meters and Cubits

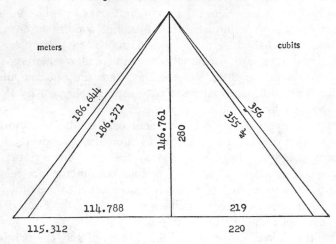

meters

cubits

186.644
186.371
146.761
280
355 ½
356
114.788
219
115.312
220

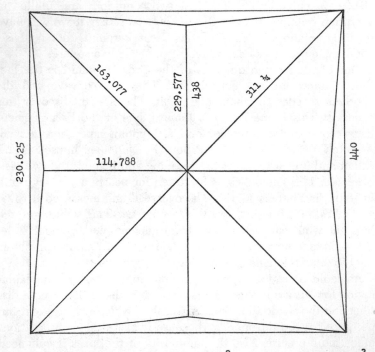

163.077
229.577
438
311 ½
230.625
114.788
440

EDGE : 219.392   BASE AREA : 53,188 M² VOLUME : 2,592,000 M³ greatly by the two semifaces forming the dihedral and thus observations of the sun, moon, and stars by the line of the apothem are made much easier. Especially this applies to observations of the stars Sirius, which was the base for the Sothic year, and Alpha Draconis, the star that was the north polar star in those days. The slight dihedral of the faces also reduces the volume of the pyramid to make it exactly 18 million cubic cubits, which for some unknown but probably religious or astronomical reason was of utmost importance to ancient Egyptians.

It is not possible now to measure the exact recession of the apothem because all the exterior stone plates have been carried away, but the dimension can be calculated with great precision. With a base of 440 cubits and a height of 280 cubits, the surface of the base has to be reduced by 743 square cubits to obtain a volume of 18 million cubic cubits. That results in shortening the apothem by 0.521 cubits and receding its base by exactly 0.844 cubits.

The most astonishing result of this arrangement is that it pushes back the two half bases of the pyramid by a quarter degree so that the two halves form an angle of ½ degree. This results in a difference of 2 minutes of solar clock time and could have served the ancient astronomers to set their water clocks or hourglasses to the exact solar time.

Let us have a look now at the angle of inclination of the faces. With the dimensions of 220 cubits and 280 cubits, the angle is 51°50'34", or 52° in round numbers, which leads to another interesting discovery. We know now that in the distant past the poles of our planet have wandered considerably. According to the latest geological data, the poles seem to stand still for a period of about 30,000 years, then move around for 6,000 years and lie still in the new place for another 30,000 years. These cycles are in harmony with the solar constant and the ice ages.

It is now estimated that the present positions of our poles were

Originally, the Pyramid of Cheops had a base side of 219.392 meters, or 418.5 cubits; a base area of 53,188 square meters, or 193,600 square cubits; and a volume of 2,592,000 cubic meters, or 18 million cubic cubits. The cubit used in this pyramid had a length of 524.148 millimeters.

established about 12,000 years ago and that they will stay put for
another 18,000 years. Let's also remember that the earth's axis
varies in cycles of about 41,000 years. With that in mind, we can
return to the Great Pyramid of Cheops.

We can assume for a moment that the Great Pyramid was constructed at a time when the inclination of the terrestrial axis was
22½° and the site of construction was at 29½° N—explaining
why the faces of the pyramid had an inclination angle of 52°.
Under these conditions the south face of the pyramid would at
the time of the winter solstice be perpendicular to the direction
of the sun, while at the summer solstice the angle would be 45°.

Now, it could very well be that the angle of 52° belonged to a
smaller and much more ancient pyramid that now is inside the
larger Great Pyramid of Cheops, a possibility indicating that the
Great Pyramid might be much older than we believe and that
Cheops was not the builder but only the enlarger of a smaller
pyramid that could be anywhere between 5,000 and 20,000 years
old. Nothing has been found so far that would allow us to determine its true age. And that might be one of the reasons why so
many people, including Napoleon, were so utterly fascinated by
this big heap of stones.

But why was the exact volume of 18 million cubic cubits so
important to the Egyptians that the writers of antiquity never
forget to mention it? I might have found an answer to this question, too, even though this may lead some to think I'm so
obsessed with the Constant of Nineveh that I seem to find it everywhere.

We know that the pyramid was built in successive steps separated by quite long periods of inactivity. This was done for good
reasons. First, the enormous weight of the construction needed
time to settle and take its final position before final corrections or
realignments could be made. The observation platform at the top
was probably used as an observatory during these building intervals to make adjustments so that the inner corridors of the pyramid would be precisely in line with the stars at certain times, especially with Sirius and Alpha Draconis which were the most
important for the Egyptian astronomers. It has been found that
3,400 years before Christ the ascending gallery was aligned with
Alpha Centauri and the descending one aimed at Alpha Dra-

conis, the polar star of that time. But the possibility exists that both these galleries could have been used similarly to sight two other stars separated by the same celestial angle several thousand years before.

Sir Gaston Maspero, director of the French archaeological mission in Egypt in the 1880s, found a curious hieroglyph in inscriptions around Sakkara. It showed a truncated pyramid with an obelisk on top of it supporting the solar disk. At first Maspero had no explanation for it. Later on, the conclusion was made that it showed the unfinished great Pyramid of Cheops at the level where the ascending gallery terminates. The Maspero hieroglyph is an indication that the work on the pyramid was interrupted for a long time at its half height.

When the Great Pyramid was at halfway mark, the surface of the platform was one quarter of the surface of its base and the volume of the pyramid to be finished was one eighth of the whole volume. The finished part therefore was seven eighths of 18 million cubic cubits, or 15.75 million cubic cubits. When you translate this latter volume into our metric system, it equals 2,268 million cubic decimeters and 2,268 million is the exact value of the Nineveh Constant. We must add here that the ancient Egyptians were quite familiar with the metric system. In the same region of Sakkara where the hieroglyph of the truncated pyramid was found, archaeologists have gathered metric standards used by ancient Egyptians. Once more we find the Great Constant but expressed in cubic decimeters. Coincidence? A coincidence is possible, of course, but I have seen so many of these coincidences that I do not believe in them any more. And then there was the discovery that the length of the granite coffer, which is not a coffin but a standard of measure placed in the king's chamber inside the Great Pyramid, is exactly 2,268 millimeters and that the total volume of the pyramid in cubic cubits multiplied by the historically sacred number 126 again gives us the number of the Great Constant: 2,268 million.

It seems that for the Egyptians, too, this number had a sacred meaning, which could mean that in different forms the Nineveh Constant was known to the entire ancient world and that it was used for thousands of years until our Sacred Mother the Church systematically destroyed all traces of earlier civilizations. Moreover, this magic number has also been discovered at Teotihuacán in Mexico.

The majority of the scientists and pyramidologists who explored the Cheops pyramid tried to discover in its dimensions all kinds of mathematical and astronomical data. Some among them even invented new units of measure to adjust their measurements to the values they wanted to obtain. It is true that many astronomical data are to be found in the dimensions of the pyramid, but the most surprising aspect is that nobody thought of a much simpler solution that seems obvious to me. Could it really be sheer coincidence that each of the eight principal dimensions of the pyramid are exact multiples of planetary conjunctions and revolution periods if we measure them with the Cheops unit of 18.719 mm, or 1/28 of an Egyptian cubit?

These eight dimensions are the perimeter of the base, the sum of the two diagonals of the base, the side of the base, the edge, the apothem, the height, and the two perpendiculars drawn from the center of the base to the edge and to the apothem. When measured in Egyptian cubits, these dimensions give us the following numbers: 49,280; 34,850; 12,320; 11,720; 9,970; 7,840; 5,840; 4,840. As anyone can verify, each of these numbers is an exact multiple of some planetary revolution or conjunction period measured in days. For example, 4,840 is equal to 55 sidereal periods or 42 synodic periods of Mercury while 5,840 represents 10 synodic periods of Venus. This can be no coincidence, no more and no less than all the other inexplicable cases where we always find the same numbers and calculation methods.

Much has been written also about the purpose for which the Great Pyramid was built. My opinion is that the basic reason for it was to serve as an astronomical observatory. Because of its enormous dimensions, the shadow of the pyramid moved very rapidly on the ground and made it possible to measure time with great accuracy. Even the year of the star Sirius was measured that way and the Egyptians figured it at 365.250681 solar days. This value was abbreviated to 365¼ days that coincided with the civil year every 1,460 years.

The Great Pyramid of Cheops was also a space beacon. Today millions of people around the world have become familiar with UFOs and the idea that space vehicles have visited our planet for eons and continue to do so, so that the possibility of space visitors does not seem so strange any more. From high above, the pyramid is visible at a very great distance to the naked eye, and in space it shows on the radar screen much farther out because of its slanted sides that reflect radar beams perpendicularly if the approach angle is 38° above horizon. It is easy to calculate that the polished stone surface of nearly 21,600 sq m is a radar reflector with a directivity factor of over 600 million for a 2-cm wave length, for example. Such a powerful reflector could have served as a beacon for the approach of a space ship and possibly has been serving for this purpose for a long time. We know that the pyramid had been painted in various colors, which could have been metalized to increase the reflectivity to laser or radar beams.

We have not yet talked about the next largest pyramid at Giza, the Pyramid of Khafre which is a true wonder of geometry and mathematics. It is built in proportions of 3:4:5 in strict adherence to the sacred triangle and the theorem of Pythagoras. The cubit which was used to lay out this pyramid's dimensions is seven sixths of the ordinary cubit because by that time Lower Egypt had been annexed to Upper Egypt and the length of the kingdom had grown to seven sixths of its previous size.

In reality, the architects who built the Pyramid of Khafre used another simpler standard—five thirds of the royal Egyptian cubit that is seven eighths of a modern meter, and this is one of the most direct correlations that I have found between the ancient measurements and the metric system. (Such is also the ancient Mycenaean 18-foot standard, that equals exactly 5 m.) To keep these measures separated, let's call the Khafre cubit the "Khafre ell" as opposed to the "Cheops cubit" that was the basic measure for the Great Pyramid.

The perimeter of the base for the Khafre Pyramid is then 984 ells, or 861 m; one side of the base itself 246 ells, or 215.25 m; the pyramid height 164 ells, or 143.5 m; and the apothem 205 ells, or 179.375 m. Each of these four dimensions can be divided by 41 to give us proportions of 3:4:5. The base area of the Khafre Pyramid is 87 per cent of that of the Cheops Pyramid and the volume 85 per cent of it, so it is not so small after all.

The smallest pyramid at Giza is the Pyramid of Menkure, the

Original Dimensions in Meters and Ells of 0.875 Meter

meters   ells

179.375   143.500   164   205

107.625   123

215.250   152.205   174

152.205   174   246

Originally, the Pyramid of Kephren had a base side of 209 meters, or
239 yards; a base area of 46,333 square meters, or 60,516 square
yards; and a volume of 2,216,240 cubic meters, or 3,308,208 cubic
yards. The special yard used has a length of 875 millimeters.

son of Cheops who was the successor of his uncle Khafre. This pyramid is about 72 m high and has a base side length of 108 m. At first glance it seems that it was built with a 30-cm foot, but precise measurements show that the unit used was the foot of 0.301835 m—a unit of length that could be more than 10,000 years old and was used also in the valley of the Indus River in Pakistan.

Measured with that foot, the Menkure Pyramid also corresponds exactly to the sacred triangle proportions and is about 22 per cent in surface and 11 per cent in volume of the Great Pyramid.

Why did Menkure build such a modest pyramid? Legends tell us that he wanted to be the "king of the people" and was disgusted by the luxury and cruelty of both his father and his uncle. To show the difference, he chose a small foot as standard for his monument instead of the royal cubit and picked a unit of length that was very ancient and half-forgotten. Menkure died very young after a reign of only eighteen years and it was probably his son Shepseskaf who finished the pyramid. The lower part is clad in red granite, and since the outer covering of pyramids was always done starting from the top while all the working ramps and scaffoldings were still in place, the bottom was the last part added to the Pyramid of Menkure, after his death.

Both the Khafre and Menkure pyramids are so perfect in their simple mathematical proportions that nobody seemed to pay much attention to them until one of the world's most prominent nuclear physicists, the 1968 Nobel prize winner professor Luis W. Alvarez, of Berkeley, California, proposed to use cosmic rays to find the hidden passages and secret chambers that everybody hoped to find in the two smaller pyramids. His plan looked very promising. Cosmic rays, discovered in 1911 by the Austrian physicist Victor Hess, would show a higher intensity if they encountered hollow passages on their way through the pyramids, and those changes would be registered by the most modern devices and analyzed by computer.

Alvarez had the full co-operation of the Egyptian government. He had all the equipment he could dream of, and the archaeological fraternity was positive Alvarez would solve the secrets of the pyramids just as they had been sure carbon dating would unlock the Mayan mysteries.

A cosmic ray detector was installed in the inner chamber of the Khafre Pyramid, which Alvarez had chosen because of its simpler structure. The general idea was to find the historical archives and scientific data hidden by the ancient Egyptian priests. Since cosmic rays penetrate even in the deepest mines and go through lead shields, the search was expected to be easy. The detector was turned in different directions to take two million readings of cosmic ray intensity changes throughout the pyramid, and the readings, registered on magnetic tape, were fed into a computer for analysis.

A modern computer installed in Cairo did the analyzing—and out came a lot of garbled nonsense. The cosmic rays were registered all right, but heavy interference from an unknown radiation source in the pyramid covered the cosmic rays with such great density that regular readings and interpretations were impossible. Not even the directions of aim could be distinguished and there was not a chance to find hidden chambers. It was a complete scientific failure.

All the equipment was dismantled and checked out again and again and it worked fine everywhere except inside the Khafre Pyramid, no matter how hard they tried. Nobody could explain it, and finally, after several futile attempts to remedy the situation, Professor Alvarez gave up and returned to California to do something more useful and controllable.

As impossible and improbable as it may seem, apparently the ancient Egyptians must have been capable of predicting the future and set up radiation barriers against us, impenetrable even to electronic scouting. It looks as if somebody or something thousands of years ago had installed electromagnetic radiation sources in at least one of the pyramids or their vicinity just to prevent the electronic devices of later generations from discovering their hidden secrets.

Another possibility, of course, is that the radiations, which many persons who spent time in pyramids or even near them claim to have felt physically, are space beacons radiating signals for astronauts in space. In any case, if indeed there is radiation, it will be possible sooner or later for us to detect it and to identify its source. For me it seems only a question of time, considering the crowds of archaeologists and other scientists from all around the world exploring the pyramids.

The interest is immense just because these secrets seem to be so well guarded. The more valuable the treasure is, the better hidden it should be. Some believe these treasures will be a fortune in gold and diamonds, but it seems much more probable that what will be found some day will be hieroglyphs inscribed on gold plates containing the whole history of man, including the true secrets of our terrestrial or astral past. And if that is so, the scientific and historical value of the records will far surpass that of the metal they are written on even if the plates were made out of platinum.

In the museum of Father Crespi in Cuenca, Ecuador, visitors can see a heavy, solid gold plate covered with hieroglyphs not yet deciphered and this plate could contain some secrets. It seems that similar plates are still hidden in caves around Cuenca, but it is difficult to obtain reliable information about these treasures and may be better not to talk much about them before one has seen these.

Legends tell us that when the Spaniards invaded their land, the Aztecs hid all their precious artifacts in caves and, as the story goes, the most valuable treasure consisted of fifty-two massive gold tablets engraved with all the history and all the sciences of the Aztec culture. It would be surprising if the Egyptians, whose land was invaded so many times by Assyrians, Greeks, Romans, and Arabs, would not have done a good job hiding their most precious belongings. Herodotus, the father of history himself, claimed that the Egyptian priests of Saïs, in Lower Egypt, told him of a secret chamber under the River Nile that would flood automatically if intruders tried to gain access to it.

In 1837 a British civil engineer, John Perring, dug down deep inside the Great Pyramid into hard rock to find the hidden chamber, but his digging was not deep enough and he found nothing. If a hidden room exists, it could have very interesting contents. Among other items, it could conceivably hide the resting place of the very first pharaoh of celestial origin and also, no doubt, a freeze generator and an electromagnetic radiation source of

PYRAMID OF CHEOPS

Secret Chamber of Herodote

```
SOUTH                                                    NORTH

CUBITS                                                   METERS
             PYRAMID
113.7                                                    59.6
             NATURAL ROCK


                    CUBIT OF  524.148 MM


         DEAD END      UNFINISHED CHAMBER    DESCENDING GALLERY

  55.1                                                   28.9

                    EXPLORED        WELL
  39.3    PRESENT NILE                                   20.6

  33.0    PERRING 1837                                   17.3


  19.6    ANCIENT NILE                                   10.3


              SECRET CHAMBER        OF HERODOTE
   0    SEA LEVEL                                          0

                    AIR AND WATER
                    UNDER PRESSURE
 - 19.6                                                  - 10.3
```

TO REDUCE THE HEIGHT OF THE CHAMBER TO 1/4 OF ITS ORIGINAL HEIGHT, AND CREATE
A PRESSURE OF 64 ATMOSPHERES, THE OUTER WATER LEVEL HAS TO GO UP 640 METERS.

This drawing shows the possible location of a secret chamber under
the Pyramid of Cheops, according to Herodotus and other ancient
writers. Because of its pyramidal shape, the outer water level would
have to rise by 640 meters and create a pressure of 64 atmospheres
to reduce the original height of the chamber to one quarter. If opened
from the top, it would be flooded.

some kind, all probably powered by changing water levels of the Nile, the cause of which for the Egyptians was the star Sothis, their name for Sirius.

As we saw from the experiences of Alvarez, some radiation source exists under the Pyramid of Khafre, and it is very probable that the hidden chamber of the priests is no figment of imagination. An indication in favor of this suspicion is the fact that no historical, scientific, or astrological documents of the ancient Egyptian priests have ever been found, even though the search goes on with the full approval of the Egyptian government, which is eager to have more of the country's glorious past discovered and revealed to the world.

Of course, modern technology plays the most important part in these archaeological explorations. Infrared photography by plane and satellite has revealed hundreds of ancient sites buried for millenniums in desert sand. One single infrared photograph taken during one of the first Apollo space missions in the 1960s uncovered more than one thousand towns, villages, canals, and highways under the desert. What can be glimpsed from space is merely the tip of the iceberg, but we can be sure that with our modern technical means much more will be discovered very soon. The methods of search are developing fast and successfully.

Meanwhile we can dig up a few things just by contemplation and reflection. When I was in Egypt studying the alignment of different monuments, I was struck by the different angle of each addition to buildings that had been made over long periods of time. Thus the temple at Karnak, adjacent to Luxor, larger than the cathedrals of Milan, Rome, Paris together, has been elongated on three occasions by new sections. The change in the longitudinal axis between the first and the last added sections is 15 degrees. And it's not hard to determine why. We know that, unlike many other calendars, the Egyptian calendar was not based on movements of the sun, the moon, or even the planets Jupiter and Saturn, but on apparent motions of the star Sirius. And this celestial reference point moves by 1 degree every 72 years, so that 15 degrees correspond to 1,080 years, or 3 times 360. That tells us that the temple at Karnak was realigned with the star Sirius once every 360 years, so that the priests could

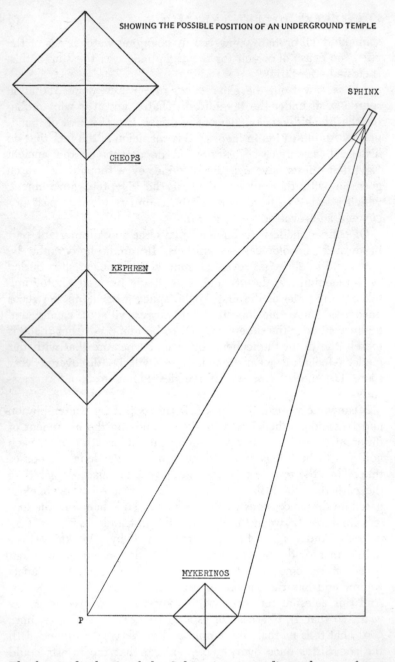

SHOWING THE POSSIBLE POSITION OF AN UNDERGROUND TEMPLE

SPHINX

CHEOPS

KEPHREN

MYKERINOS

P

The longitudinal axis of the Sphinx intersects diagonal axes of two of the pyramids. The point of intersection, P, might indicate the location of an underground temple containing the astronomical and mathematical secrets of the Egyptians, which have never been discovered.

maintain their line of vision on certain stars or constellations on certain days of the solar year.

One thousand and eighty years is one tenth of the great year of the Babylonians and the Hindus, and the 108-year cycle of the Rosicrucians is one hundredth of the 10,800-year Great Cycle. This international fraternity devoted to the application of religious mysticism to modern life, alternates its secret activities with public action every 108 years. So it was secret from 1807 till 1915 and will close its present public period in 2023.

To come back to the hidden treasures of the pharaohs, let's examine the map of Giza, a western suburb of Cairo, where the three pyramids and the Sphinx are situated. The diagonals of the Cheops and Khafre pyramids both run on the same axis northeast to south-west, and one of the diagonals of the Menkure Pyramid cuts the alignment of the other two pyramids at a given point P. When we observe now the geometrical center of the Sphinx, we find that it can be aligned with the southern face of the Khafre Pyramid, which has its special significance. More importantly, however, this alignment is at an angle of 15 degrees with the central axis of the Sphinx. When this axis is continued west it cuts the extensions of the diagonals of all the three pyramids at the same point P that we found above.

It could be a coincidence, but if I were looking for the lost treasures of ancient Egypt, P is the spot where I would start digging.

CHAPTER 4

The Maltese Cross

ETHNOLOGISTS CONSIDER THE Aegean Sea between Greece, the Island of Crete, and Turkey to be the cradle of our Western civilization that started 4,000 years ago as the Cretan and Mycenaean cultures. Everybody knows that. But few are aware that 5,000 years before Crete and Mycenae prospered, civilized people lived in small villages and towns of Anatolia in Turkey and some of these places, like Dorak in the northern part of Anatolia, were famous before Troy was built. The tools and arms of these people were made of obsidian, a black volcanic glass that they also polished into mirrors. Cattle was raised and cereals grown there 9,000 years ago.

How could the inhabitants of this region become civilized so early? We can find the answer if we are willing to accept the discovery that these early humans used even more surprising knowledge than animal husbandry and agriculture, namely, astronomy and mathematics.

In the center of the Aegean Sea exists a small island by the name of Delos. It has always been considered the most sacred place of ancient Greece, even though no one seemed to know why, of all places, Delos should be so sacred. It was simply an accepted belief apparently carried over from a past unknown. To me it seems there can be only one logical explanation for this belief. Delos is the geometric center of a true design of the gods—

the Maltese cross of majestic proportions that extends over hundreds of miles over the Aegean Sea, Greece, and Turkey.

To show that this gigantic geometric figure is not the figment of imagination and no science-fiction invention, please follow me in tracing this cross with a compass and a straightedge over a good map of the Aegean Sea. Let's put the sharp point of one compass arm in the middle of Delos and measure a radius of 1,500 ancient Egyptian stadia, or 270 km, and run the trace arm of the compass full circle. We will have passed in succession through Cape Matapan and Delphi in Greece; the island of Psathura in the Northern Sporades; Antandrus and Sardis in Anatolia; Camirus on Rhodes; and Akra and Araden on Crete.

Now let's trace a smaller circle with Delos still in the center. A radius of 1,000 Egyptian stadia, or 180 km, will give a ring that connects Hermione in Greece; a high bank between the islands of Lesbos and Skyros; Didyma in Anatolia; and a point now submerged north of the Dia Island. Thus, if we include Delos, we have thirteen geographical sites that have always been sacred places marked by temple ruins constructed over even more ancient ruins from time immemorial. Thirteen has always been a magic number for astrological reasons. All the places that we have found tracing the circles around Delos are not on firm land, but we must remember that in the past the Mediterranean had a much lower water level. At any rate, these sites were not chosen by chance as our next step of tracing on the map will prove.

When we connect all the sites with straight lines going from point to point in the following order: Delos, Matapan, Hermione, Delphi, Delos, Psathura, Lesbos, Antandrus, Delos, Sardis, Didyma, Camirus, Delos, Akra, Dia, Araden, and Delos we have drawn the magnificent geometrical figure known as the "Maltese cross," a sacred pagan sign since antiquity as well as the sign of the Crusaders who fought to liberate Jerusalem from the Infidels. Indeed, the designs of the Lord are beyond human comprehension!

What interests us now is how and why such a gigantic pattern was marked on the Aegean and surrounding lands. I do not believe that even today's land surveyors could so precisely mark such a gigantic figure of over 360 miles jumping from island to island and stretching over sea and mountains. Except from high

THE MALTESE CROSS OF THE AEGEAN SEA

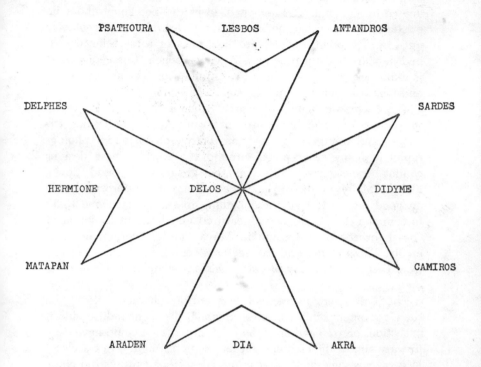

A beautiful Maltese cross centered on the island of Delos and 540 kilometers wide, can be obtained by tracing lines between thirteen famous Greek temples around the Aegean Sea, but ancient Greeks did not know it. Was that cross traced by astronauts from outer space several thousand years ago?

up in the air this Maltese cross would not be visible. To measure and mark all the salient points, two very modern tools of mapping are an absolute necessity. First, a fixed-position space satellite that turns synchronously at the Delos latitude of 37°23′ with a ground velocity of 1,328 km ph. Then, to keep the capsule stationary over Delos, one of our newest devices that was perfected only a short time ago—a navigation and distance-measuring ground radar with metallic reflectors installed at distances of 180 and 270 km around the two circles.

The Maltese cross of the Aegean must have been constructed by just such means or with other much better devices still unknown to mankind. The ancient Greeks did not know about its existence and they had no knowledge of astronomy or geometry until the Egyptians gave them the basics of these sciences. To find out for what purpose and to whose benefit this geometrical marking was set up, we have to continue our logical deductions and look back many, many thousands of years.

The geometric figures of Nasca in Peru that have been described in dozens of books are not so unique. Straight lines, triangles, and trapezoids have been discovered by aerial photography in many other places around the world. These designs cannot be recognized while your feet are on the ground. Some, like the Maltese cross of the Aegean Sea, can be perceived only on good maps. And all these baffling markings have one thing in common—they have been measured and laid out in stadia of 600 ft, or 180 m, the same in Mayan and Egyptian measurements. These stadia and the feet and cubits that were derived from them are the very oldest prehistoric standards of measurement.

The Maltese cross presents a very curious characteristic. When the eight outer points are set on a circle, the eight radii divide it in sections of 3/28 and of 4/28 of the circle. That could have been just a whim of the creators of this geometric figure, but a closer look reveals some hidden meaning. In ancient cultures the circle has been divided in 5 or 6 and 7 parts, in 8, 12, and 360 sectors. The Arabs seem to have used 11 and 44 parts, but as far as we know nobody in classical antiquity divided a full circle in 28 sectors. However, if we cross the Atlantic and go to the Mayas, Incas, or even the Wyoming Indians, we find this division. The Medicine Wheel of Wyoming was divided into 28 equal parts and the temple of Tiahuanaco in Bolivia, was divided into 28 sectors by 29 columns. Also the cubit of Cuenca, in Ecuador, has 7 hands of 4 fingers each, or a total of 28 fingers, because the gods of that time had only 4 fingers on each hand as many sculptures and drawings show it. Twenty-eight times two is 56, and such is the number of hieroglyphs on the solid gold plate of

Cuenca. Note also that megalithic Stonehenge, in Wiltshire, England, has 56 Aubrey holes. In the classical antique world only the royal cubit of the Egyptians was divisible by 7 hands of 4 fingers each, and that brings us to the possible conclusion that the Egyptians, as well as the creators of Stonehenge and the Maltese cross, had a connection or a common origin with the civilizations of Cuenca, Tiahuanaco, and Wyoming.

There are ancient Greek temples and cities that have been submerged by the Mediterranean. Today nobody has a right to doubt that reality. Aerial photography has rediscovered what old Aegean fishermen found thousands of years ago—sunken temples, villages, and streets. Just outside the small port of Halieis, between Mycenae and Tiryns, there reposes under many feet of water a former temple of Zeus built in 780 B.C. Just like the Karnak temple near Luxor, it was rebuilt several times, with new additions reoriented at angles up to 40 degrees from the origin, representing a time span of 2,880 years, or 10 times 288 years, the Tiahuanaco number. That means the oldest part of this temple was constructed 5,600 years ago. The building at Halieis is constructed in Mycenean feet of 0.277 m, which for all practical purposes equals the foot of the Celts, or 0.276 m. This same measure was employed in the megalithic sites of England, France, and Spain, which according to the latest estimates date back 10,000 years or more, preceding the ziggurats of Mesopotamia and the Egyptian pyramids.

All the legends of Mediterranean people mention the cataclysmic variations in the level of the sea and the eruption of a volcano on the island of Thera, probably in about 1500 B.C., or 3,500 years ago. The explosion and the following tidal waves destroyed the Minoan civilization. Many islands around Crete disappeared under water and the bottom of the sea caved in. The conquest of the Aegean Islands by Mycenaeans from Greece followed. But before this catastrophe, about 12,000 years ago, there was the really big one—the flooding of the Gibraltar Strait by the Atlantic Ocean, and the sudden rise of the Mediterranean Sea level by at least 200 m, or 600 ft.

Modern calculations have been made to see what would happen to the Mediterranean if the Strait of Gibraltar were dammed up. All the rivers that bring fresh water to the Mediterranean could not equal the volume of water evaporated by the heat of the sun and the sea level would descend rather rapidly, reducing the evaporation area and finally settling at a point of equilibrium where the water flowing in from the rivers would equal the amount evaporating. This new level would be about 600 ft below the present level. The past would return. The islands of the Aegean Sea would be much larger and all thirteen points of the Maltese cross would be visible.

When the isthmus of Gibraltar gave way to the pressure of the Atlantic because some cosmic event caused the northern polar ice cap to melt and raised the level of the oceans, all the coastal lines of Greece and its islands were inundated and whole civilizations disappeared. A few ignorant shepherds high in the mountains survived and carried over to future generations legends of this deluge. But all was not lost. The arid mountains were now closer to the sea and the climate changed. With more frequent rains, agriculture prospered and domestic animals grew fatter. This may well have been the time of Paradise on earth, as the Hebrew legends recall it. It may have been the period chosen by the Bible as the starting point for the cultural evolution of man by simply ignoring all previous civilizations. Most certainly what the Bible calls the Garden of Eden is the Golden Age of Mediterranean legend.

But legends are usually not simple inventions. Most of them are based on historical facts precisely dated, sometimes in very esoteric terms. The legend of Hercules, the strong and brave Greek hero who won immortality by performing the twelve heroic labors demanded by Hera, is a good example. In this tale of antiquity we find the lion of Nemea, the hydra of Lerna, the pillars of Hercules, and the bull of Crete. Translating these into the signs of the zodiac we have the Lion, the Crab, the Twins, and the Bull. For the astrologers of the Mediterranean basin, the cycle of precession of the equinoxes, a revolution of the earth's axis around the pole of the ecliptic, was 25,920 years divided into twelve periods of 2,160 years each. Assuming that our modern astrologers finally agree where we are at the present time on the zodiac, we can assume that the era of the Fishes started on March 21 in the first year after Christ. In that case, the zodiacal era of the Lion started in 10,800 B.C.; that of the Crab in 8640 B.C.; that of the Twins in 6480 B.C.; that of the Bull in 4320 B.C.; and that of the Ram (or the Golden Fleece) in 2160 B.C., ending at the start of the present era of the Fishes. Consequently, we can assume that the Hercules legends indicate that the collapse of the land between the promontories at Ceuta in Africa and Gibraltar in Europe happened about 12,000 years ago, and it took nearly 6,000 years for the flood waters to settle at the present level.

It is not necessary, however, to go to Greece or South America to find geometric designs and alignments of mysterious origin. In England surveyors long ago found that nearly all megalithic monuments repose on lines of magnetic or telluric flux, or ley lines, as the English call these pathways. These ley lines, when photographed from high altitude show up quite clearly as they can be detected by lusher vegetation and electromagnetic radiations interfering with radio waves. Also exposures on photographic film over these ley lines tend to get fogged by some radiation. Like avenues converging in Paris at the Arc de Triomphe, so these magnetic boulevards intersect at important megalithic monuments of great fame and past glory. And UFOs frequently follow these lines in their flights.

Four of these lines run parallel from east to west through England, France, and Spain at 42°, 45°, 48°, and 51° north latitude and at a distance of 333.333 m from each other, so that the most southern line is separated from the most northern by exactly 1,000 km. That seems surprising since, according to established science, the metric system was not known to prehistoric man. But on the English ley line at 51° we find situated such sites as Glastonbury, Stonehenge, Avebury, and Canterbury. The line in France at 48° north latitude intersects Chartres, Domrémy, Sainte-Odile, and other sites that are well known for ancient cathedrals and remarkable monuments. The 45° line runs through Les Eyzies, Lascaux, and Le Puy—a region that is considered one of the most valuable repositories of prehistoric sites anywhere in the world. The caves of Lascaux and Les Eyzies are well known but it is possible that still much more will be discovered there in the future. The 42° north latitude line in Spain starts near Noya on the Atlantic Ocean, where the refugees of sunken Atlantis probably came to land and runs through Santiago de Compostela, Burgos, and the Logroño, and Roncesvalles —all historic sites of ancient fame.

In France, too, several other mysterious lines exist that act just like their counterparts in England and are followed by UFOs in flight. These lines do not form geometric figures like the Maltese cross in the Aegean, nor do they show up like the designs in Nasca, Peru, but they are most interesting even though nobody has discovered exactly what they represent, since they form a huge triangle.

About 15 km north of Sedan there stands a megalithic monument called the Giant's Grave. When a line is traced on a map from this monument straight south for 700 km till it reaches Istres in Provence, it goes through an unbelievable number of historical sites, from dolmens and menhirs of prehistoric times to cloisters and castles of the Middle Ages. Another such line dotted with megaliths drawn 76° west of the Giant's Grave–Istres line about 700 km stops in Quimper, on the coast of Brittany. When the two lines are connected by a third to form a triangle, that line goes through the most concentrated assembly of dolmens, menhirs, and cromlechs in the world—the region of Carnac in Brittany. Is there a connection with Karnak, in Egypt? The names sound alike, but as far as I know, nobody yet has found the common denominator.

Other surprises keep piling up when we continue to analyze this gigantic triangle of France. If a fourth line is drawn from the Giant's Grave to the center of the base between Provence and Brittany it is just as rich in ruins of antiquity as the two sides of the triangle. The triangle has now an apex of 76°, two side angles of 52° each, two sides of 700 km, a base of 865 km, and a height of 550 km. Hold on to your hats—you have the exact same proportions and angles as the Great Pyramid of Cheops! The Triangle of France is exactly 14 million times bigger than the area of the cross section of the Cheops Pyramid. The surface of this triangle is 238,000 sq km, and the area of the circle into which the Aegean Maltese cross could be placed is 238,000 sq km, which is the same. Can you believe that we have here again a simple coincidence?

The Triangle of France is not the only example having dimensions that are proportional to those of the Great Pyramid. The

A huge triangle, proportional to the dimensions of the Great Pyramid of Cheops but 14 million times larger, can be traced within the borders of France. Each side of the triangle is lined up with prehistoric and historic monuments, but the French did not know it. Could it also have been traced by ancient astronauts like the Maltese cross of the Aegean Sea?

tiny pyramid of Falicon on a mountain above Nice, built in 1260 by Crusaders who had returned from Jerusalem, is exactly 1/288 the scale of Cheops. This number, 288, is known to us from the Temple of Kalasasaya in Tiahuanaco and its calendar year of 288 days. Why the Crusaders who built the pyramid in Falicon chose this scale of 1/288 is not known but the precise proportions with the Great Pyramid should not surprise anybody because the Crusaders on their way and back from Jerusalem passed the original one.

Much more surprising is the study made of some of the great cathedrals in France and their mathematical structure, where again astounding similarities with the Great Pyramid of Cheops crop up. The monumental cathedral of Chartres shows the same constants and proportions as the pyramid and, above all, seems to be of much older age in its original foundations taken over from a previous pagan temple on the same site. The standard foot of Chartres that was used to construct the cathedral was 0.3684 m. The length of a longitude degree at Chartres is 73,680 m, exactly 200,000 of these feet.

The most surprising derivative of this dimension is the cubic foot of Chartres. It equals 50 liters or 50 kg of water—when there was no metric system!

The cathedral of Reims is farther north than Chartres and there the dimension of the basic foot is 0.3557 m, also proportional to the local latitude, and the cubic foot weight is 45 liters or kg of water; but this is the Russian standard unit of weight called *pood*.

The cathedrals of France have another mystery in the pattern of their placement. If you paste over the map of France little gold stars in Abbeville, Amiens, Bayeux, Chartres, Évreux, Laon, Le Mans, Paris, Reims, and Rouen, where the most famous cathedrals stand in the middle of the cities, you have the same configuration as the stars in the constellation of Virgo. The main star in Virgo is Spica; this brilliant star has always been venerated as the goddess of fertility and maternity. In the group of cathedrals Spica is Reims. Again I have difficulty dismissing this symbolism as an accident and coincidence. Religion has always been the twin sister of astrology.

But I would like to come back once more to the giant trian-

IN METERS, CHARTRES INCHES OF 23.0625 MM, AND CHEOPS FINGERS OF 18.7195 MM

NORTH

PYRAMID

36.465 M
1581 I
1948 F

32.616 M
1414 I
1742 F

16.308 M
707 I
871 F

32.616 M
1414 I
1742 F

23.063 M
1000 I
1232 F

26.023 M
1128 I
1390 F

Total length – 110.700 M – 4800 I – 5914 F

Length of the nave – 73.800 M – 3200 I – 3942 F

AREA OF EACH TABLE

5,318,789	square centimeters	or	531.8789	square meters
1,000,000	square inches	or	3906	square feet
1,517,824	square fingers	or	1936	square cubits

or 1/100 of the area of Cheops Pyramid

The floor plan of the Chartres cathedral is based on three tables, a round one, a square one, and a rectangular one. Each of these tables has exactly the same area, which is one hundredth of that of the Great Pyramid of Cheops. The area of each table is 531.88 square meters while that of the Great Pyramid is 53,188 square meters. A special Chartres inch of 23.0625 millimeters, representing one ten-thousandth of the side of the Pyramid, was used for the construction but the Church did not know it. Who did actually design the Chartres cathedral in 1194 and build it in twenty-six years according to the size of the Great Pyramid?

gles. The map of Egypt shows two of them so far never noticed. The vertical axis of Lower Egypt is the line drawn from Bedet to Kubra to Giza while the horizontal axis goes through Saïs to Kubra and Mendes. If we now construct the northern triangle Saïs to Bedet to Mendes we have exact distances of 400, 300, and 300 stadia of 180 m. The southern triangle Saïs to Giza to

THE VIRGO CONSTELLATION AND FRENCH CATHEDRALS

THE RELATIVE POSITIONS OF THE STARS
ARE THE SAME AS THOSE OF THE CATHEDRA

The relative positions of the ten major cathedrals in France are the same as those of ten stars in the Virgo constellation, over a distance of 300 kilometers, although there were no maps in France 800 years ago. Did ancient astronauts determine the locations of these sites long before the construction of the cathedrals? Again, the Church did not know that.

Mendes measures 400, 650, and 650 stadia. Now let's jump to the American continents and measure the distances between three religious centers of the ancient Mayas—Copán (Honduras), La Venta (Mexico), and Chichén Itzá (Mexico). Each of the sides of this triangle is 3,600 Mayan stadia of 180 m each. Yes, the same 180 m as that of the Egyptian stadia! This cannot be a coincidence. The distances on another Mayan pattern—a trapeze between four religious centers Teotihuacán, Chichén Itzá, La Muralla, and Monte Albán are 2,000, 4,000, 6,000 stadia of 180 m each, but the biggest of the figures, the South American triangle between Nasca, Tiahuanaco, and the caves of Cuenca, measure 3,750, 7,500, and 10,000 Tiahuanaco stadia of 178 m adjusted to the local latitude and therefore shorter than the previous by less than 2 m.

The most logical explanation for these triangles is that they were navigational patterns for spaceship landings, very similar to the re-entry corridors we calculate today for our space missions. For me, who has seen many such patterns drawn theoretically in the Pacific for our Apollo missions, the analogy is overwhelming.

And there are other reasons why such speculation is not at all impossible. First, we have all the legends in folklore and religious records from around the world attesting to the theory. Then we have paintings, engravings, and sculptures showing the celestial visitors descending in flaming chariots that look just like retro-rockets firing; there are even bronze figurines of astronauts.

Now, some legends indicate that space visitors came from the planet Venus. That too is not impossible. Much of the information we have today points in that direction. First, Venus is unique among planets in that it spins clockwise. Mercury, earth, Mars, Jupiter, Saturn, and the rest spin counterclockwise, which makes scientists think of Venus as an alien who drifted from outer space into our solar system and was captured by the gravitational field of our sun. On its way to solar orbit it nearly brushed our earth, and in doing so, both Venus and earth synchronized their rotation and revolution periods. The Mayas had discovered that 2,920 days represents 5 synodic periods and 13 sidereal periods of Venus, as well as 8 sidereal periods of the earth. Venus has the same face turned to earth every time. They line up after 584 days. In my opinion, that could be a proof that Venus almost got captured by our planet but its velocity and mass were too great, so that eventually it established a closer and faster orbit around the Sun. There was, however, a moment when the Venusians could have landed on earth as easily as we landed on the moon. And that may have been when the first missions established markers and glide patterns in suitable locations like the plains of Nasca, the highlands of Tiahuanaco, and the Mexican jungle. When, after a while, the newly arrived got accustomed to our air and water they showed themselves to the local inhabitants, who promptly accorded them the rank of gods and many different names like Kukulcan, Uiracocha, Orejona, Taaroa, Maoui, and even Elohim, the Hebrew name of God in our Bible.

The question is when did this happen. Two dates are possible —the first great flood 12,000 years ago and the last inundation of our earth about 6,000 years ago. As far as I know, there are no records about the existence of Venus in our skies that would be older than 5,000 years. However, I am skeptical about this date because there are still enormous quantities of manuscripts and books of very old age that have not been read or translated or even discovered, and any day now we could find a proof that 12,000 years ago Venus entered our skies like a gigantic comet and created cataclysms of a fantastic scale all over the world.

What conclusions are possible from the facts presented in this chapter? First, the biblical idea that our culture started only 6,000 years ago in the Middle East is false. Very intelligent and capable humans lived in Tiahuanaco, in Bolivia, where the ruins are 30,000 years old. The caves of Cuenca (Ecuador), Lascaux (France), and Altamira (Spain) must have at least 20,000 years to look back on. The Maltese cross with its temples is probably 12,000 years old, older than the agricultural centers of Dorak and Hacilar in Anatolia. The lost continent of Atlantis sank into the deep in the year 9564 B.C. if we want to believe the Tibetans, or it happened 11,500 years ago according to the Egyptian priests who told it to Solon, one of whose descendants told it to Plato.

For very good reasons, ethnologists have concluded that the earthlings of 30,000 years ago were not highly developed. But we have seen that around that time astounding knowledge was demonstrated on several continents, always in the same basic style. And this can make sense only if we are willing to accept the theory of visiting space gods, that it was astronauts who caused the great change by insemination and selective mutation, thus creating a new hybrid human race adapted to climate and living conditions on earth while retaining at least some of the high intelligence and knowledge of the original visitors. The Elohims accomplished their mission well.

CHAPTER 5

The Rhodes Calculator

MOST SENSATIONAL discoveries happen by chance, perhaps because of what we may call the benevolent intervention of the gods, as long as there is no better explanation for it. And one such haphazard revelation that simultaneously revolutionized archaeology and the history of science and technology occurred in October 1900, without anybody noticing it.

It was the finding by Aegean fishermen of the Rhodes calculator, or the computer of Antikythera on an ancient sunken Roman ship. It changed all our ideas about the history of science. It also started a new science—underwater archaeology—and since I was one of the very first addicts of the aqualung and deep-sea diving from the times when all equipment was handmade by the dedicated few themselves, let me tell you about this discovery in a little more detail.

On that day in October of 1900 a Greek tartan, a large, single-masted Mediterranean ship with a large lateen sail, returning from a diving expedition along the African coast where it had been gathering sponges, ran into a stiff southwester and had to look for a harbor to let the gale blow over. It was a typical Greek sponge fishermen's rig. Captain Demetrios Condos, a seasoned veteran of sponge diving, knew that the straits between the islands of Crete and Antikythera was one of the worst places to be in a storm. So he pulled fast into the port of Potamos at the northern tip of Antikythera island. There, guarded by the enormous bulk of the Glyphalda Cape he found calm water.

The Greeks are charming people whom I love very much, but when they have nothing else to do they can't stop drinking, gambling, and fighting. And the trouble is that they seem to have very little to do far too often. That is exactly what happened to Condos and his crew of twelve. The storm lasted for days, and to keep both his tartan and his diving boat, where the air pump and the diving suits were kept, from being turned into shambles by his wine-loving crew, Condos sent all of them on a wild goose chase—to look for sponges along the shelf of Cape Glyphalda. He could not care less whether they found sponges or not. He had to keep them occupied.

In the gray of the early morning, while the gale was still blowing in the open sea, the diving boat left the tartan in the port of Potamos and was rowed to Pinakakia, where the water was calm and clear and good for diving. Captain Condos looked through his glass-bottom pail set in the water and could see down about 30 fathoms to a protruding ledge. Thirty fathoms is about 180 feet, which is the outer limit for a diver in an air-pump suit, but Condos' divers were probably among the world's best at that time and he figured he could try his luck and keep his men busy by sending them down one after another at five-minute intervals. Six divers could explore the bottom for half an hour while the other six would man the oars and the air pump.

Diving is very dangerous business and Condos' men knew it. The six divers stood assembled in the bow of the diving boat, smoking one cigarette after another to calm down hunger pains. Nobody had eaten breakfast because food in the stomach increases the chance of contracting cramps, the terror of all divers. One after another they flipped their cigarettes in the water, soaped their wrists with black soap so that the diving-suit cuffs would close airtight, and with the help of the youngest boy on the boat, an apprentice seaman, put on their cumbersome diving equipment. When the deck boy had rinsed out each helmet with sea water and cleansed the visor glass with a special sponge to prevent fogging, the casque was screwed on to the diver's suit, and after some weights were added to his breastplate and the

soles of his boots, the diver at the end of the air tube was on his
way to the deep.

The lead weights which pulled them down were good old
historic metal, mostly from Roman foundries. All Roman ships
used wooden anchors, some as many as six, with lead crossbars, and the standard Roman galley had as much as 2 or 3
tons of lead. Mediterranean fishermen and divers had divested
the sunken wrecks long ago of every scrap of metal to build their
own boats and anchors, and the Condos vessel was no exception.

The historic moment started when the second in command on
the boat, Mercurio, gave order to one of the oldest divers, Elias
Stadiatis, to plop into the water. The deck boy called out loud
the air-pump manometer readings, and when the needle indicated 15 fathoms a sand hourglass was turned over to time the
descent for another full minute. When sand ran out, the depth of
the shelf was reached and the pump pressure indicated a depth
of 30 fathoms—the limit at which a diver can work for five minutes. But Stadiatis did not stay down his allocated time. A few
moments after reaching the bottom he yanked the descent cord
in panic and started his ascent. Condos and Mercurio both ran to
help him get out, because no old, experienced diver would do
such a thing unless there was real danger or emergency. When
Statiatis' face appeared through the visor of the helmet he
looked like a corpse, pale and with bulging eyes. The metal
casque came off and Stadiatis could barely speak. He stammered
something about naked women and horses but was otherwise in-
coherent. He mentioned the Holy Virgin in the same breath and
made no sense.

Finally Condos got mad and ordered him to calm down and
tell exactly what had happened. Stadiatis did his best, but that
wasn't much. He insisted that many horses, naked women, and
women in flowing robes were on the bottom and that most of the
pretty faces were pock-marked. Captain Condos was a calm and
practical man and would not buy this fool's story. So he put on
his own diving suit and went down himself. Mercurio was hold-
ing the descent line, and after a minute of descent he felt one
strong pull—the signal to slacken the cable and that everything
was all right.

The captain stayed down for only a few minutes, not using up all his time. When his helmet was unscrewed he looked very satisfied, even smug, but did not say a word to anybody. He simply ordered his cable basket pulled up and in it the astonished crew saw a green metallic human hand, hollow and full of sand. Then Condos let loose his best salty sea language and called all his crew and Stadiatis especially the dumbest idiots that ever sailed the Mediterranean. He told them that down under there was a whole ship full of stone and bronze statues! A sunken treasure.

Up to this point the history of this event is clear and simple, but not so, further on. The official version of the authorities and the stories of the crew are quite different. To understand this discrepancy, we have to talk a little about the Greek sponge fishermen, particularly from the Aegean. First of all, they are great divers, who can stand and survive water pressure down to 180 feet for several minutes. Anything of value that could be retrieved from such depth is their prey. Flooded houses and sunken galleys have been mines of gold, silver, copper, bronze, and lead. As I mentioned before, a Roman galley usually had as many as six big wooden anchors with crossbars of lead, and one single shipwreck could yield two or three tons of this valuable metal. Condos and his crew would not let their prize of naked women and horses drift away, not if these statues were made of precious metal that could be sold with no questions asked.

Condos became a rich man, for a while at least. He ordered a new bigger ship built for himself and started smuggling arms across the Mediterranean, mostly French army rifles. He wanted to be a big businessman and went broke. His ship was sold for debts, and he had to return to the sea and dive for sponges until the cramps got him and he became half paralyzed. He died in 1926 in the home of his daughter, who had given him his last shelter in Suez, in Egypt. The gods had abandoned the man who once was so lucky.

But to return to that time in October 1900, off Antikythera after Condos had cleared the wreck of anything valuable that he could lift out and sold it, he informed the owners of his tartan, the Lyndiakos brothers, about the wreck off Antikythera and suggested that the Greek government should be informed and put in charge of the salvage operation of this historic sunken art, which was to be presented as his patriotic gift to Greece. It was done, and Condos felt great. His own home was on the Dodecanese island of Syme, at that time ruled by Turks, whom Condos hated. As you see, history does not change. The problem of the Greeks and the Turks is the same today as it was seventy-eight years ago.

The Greek government ordered its navy to carry out the salvage of the statues on the sunken ship. It was done the military way: get things done fast no matter how. Big crane ships arrived, and the divers pushed over the coastal shelf on which the treasure ship rested all the big stone blocks from the deck of the galley that hindered the divers from getting at the bronze statues. Nobody noticed that the big stone blocks were huge statues turned upside down so that the square sockets alone were visible to the officer in charge of the operation. When this mistake was finally noticed, orders were given to retrieve without fail everything that was on or inside the sunken ship. The museum of Athens received the whole lot—the stone sculptures, the bronze figures, a heap of broken bronze heads and arms, and some lumps of indefinite shape that would be sorted out later. By the end of summer in 1901 the sunken galley was nothing but an empty hulk, 100 feet long and 40 feet wide, the standard measurements for a Roman galley of 83 B.C. And this wreck remained there totally abandoned for another fifty-two years until 1953 when Captain Jacques Cousteau and his divers visited it.

But meanwhile, back in 1902, a young Greek student by the name of Valerio Stais had been sorting the broken pieces of bronze at the National Museum in Athens. His task was to find and match missing heads and arms so that the sculptures could be restored, but he noticed a calcified lump of bronze that did not fit anywhere and was not part of a statue. While drying, the calcified mass had split in half and what was visible looked like the insides of a big watch—gears and pinions and dials with inscriptions in ancient Greek characters and signs of the zodiac. Valerio Stais guessed that it must be an astronomical clock of some sort or an instrument of navigation; he wrote a paper to announce this finding to the scientific world, with the result that he was declared to be a fool. The date of the sunken galley was indicated by artifacts in several places on the ship. It was without any doubt determined to be the year 83 B.C., and everybody knew that at that time there were no clocks—or any other device —made with gears. Neither were mechanical calculators constructed in ancient Greece.

To tell time, both Greeks and Romans of the last century before Christ used sun dials, water-dripping *clepsydras,* or handy sand hourglasses. Never before had anybody found or read of gear and dial mechanisms for that purpose. Besides, nobody in that century was rushed, and, except for astronomers, nobody seemed much concerned about keeping the exact time. (Night and day were divided into twelve parts each and only at the spring and the autumnal equinoxes were the divisions of equal length.)

Thus the conclusion of the scholars was that the mechanism found in the galley of Antikythera simply could not have been made 2,000 years ago. It had to be a clock perhaps 200 or 300 years old, tossed overboard by the captain of a ship passing over the wreck of the ancient galley. That was an explanation acceptable to the twentieth-century scientific establishment, and for the next fifty-six years nobody had the nerve to speak about it again. To avoid controversy, the find was registered in the museum catalogue as an astrolabe, and that's where things rested more or less until 1958, when a young English mathematician, Dr. Derek J. de Solla Price, working at the Princeton Institute of Advanced Study, obtained a grant to study the Antikythera mechanism and later published his findings in the scientific magazines *Natural History* and *Scientific American.*

Luckily, the museum technicians had taken good care of the clock remnants. There were four main pieces, each composed of many layers of bronze gears and some smaller lumps. Some parts were missing and probably still on the bottom of the Aegean. As he studied what was there, Price had the good idea to use radiations with different intensities and frequencies to photograph separate layers of the mechanism that could not be taken apart. These layers were minuscule, about 2 millimeters thick each, and all together there were as many as thirty different gears. This method of selective photography also proved that the clock contained a differential gear—a sensational discovery indicating a very high technological achievement, since differential gears have been invented only in very recent times, to make it possible to compute the sum or difference of two angular velocities with gears.

The differential mechanism of the Antikythera clock is of the flat type. It consists of one big crown gear, a pinion in the center, and satellite gears between the pinion and the crown. These satellites are mounted on a rotating support that moves with an angular speed representing the difference between those of the big crown and pinion. For somebody who lived 2,000 years ago to have built this mechanism would really have been a superb achievement. The size of the whole calculator must have been equal to that of a portable typewriter of today, with two dials in the back and one in the front. This front dial had two concentric bands—one with the signs of the zodiac and the other, a movable one, with names of each month in Greek. A pointer that was moved by the mechanism indicated the position of the sun in the zodiac for each day of the year.

The two dials in the back seemed to indicate the phases of the moon and the movements of the five planets known at that time —Mercury, Venus, Mars, Jupiter, and Saturn. The mechanism was set in motion by a worm gear that had to be rotated by one turn every day, probably at noon. The last information available about this calculator is that it may have had five dials, two in the front and three in the back, and that all of them were adjustable.

This discovery was revolutionary in every sense of the word. Many called the Antikythera clock a computer because the purpose of the gadget was probably to avoid tedious astronomical computations. Price himself said in a scientific meeting in Washington that finding a thing like this computer in a Roman galley was like finding a jet plane in King Tutankhamen's tomb.

The probable builder of this astronomical calculator must have been the Greek astronomer, mathematician, and philosopher Geminus who was the apprentice of Posidonius. The birth and death dates of Geminus are not known, but his teacher, Posidonius, a philosopher of the Stoic school founded by Zeno, lived from 135 to 51 B.C., and taught on the island of Rhodes.

Geminus was a near contemporary of his master in philosophy and became famous through his manuals of astronomy and mathematics. He also invented most of all known combinations of gears, the worm gear, the differential gear, the bevel gear and probably also the crank and connecting rod that transforms uniform circular motion into alternating linear movement. If there was at that time somebody in Greece who could have been able to build the calculator of Rhodes, it was Geminus. Only he could have had the idea to put together differential gears with bevel gears and connecting rods and mathematical and astronomical dials in a single box to make a navigational computer. The complicated mechanism of more than thirty separate gears was probably put together by his pupils—all Greek masters of that time had apprentices.

The date for which this calculator was set for the last time is the year 86 B.C., as can be seen by the relative positions of the dials and pointers. The Roman galley which was transporting the statues from Rhodes to Rome probably sank near Antikythera three years later, in 83 B.C.

And the year 86 B.C. was a remarkable date. There were five conjunctions of planets in four zodiacal signs that year, an ideal time to set an astronomical calculator precisely if it was already built or to start constructing one. So here we have another trailblazing achievement of the famous Greeks, permitting the Graecophils once more to claim that all science came from Greece.

Unfortunately not all people agree on that, and I am one who disagrees. In recent years one discovery after another has shown that all the scientific knowledge of Greeks was inherited and borrowed from the high priests of Egypt, who had obtained it thousands of years earlier from an unknown source. The calculator of Rhodes can give us some indication where this mysterious unknown source of all science was located or at least it can indicate the direction in which we will have to look for the beginning of our civilization.

If somebody wants to construct an astronomical calculator by using intermeshing gears, the first condition is to find the number of cycles necessary to obtain an exact number of whole days. Some of these cycles are easily found but many are nearly impossible. A good example is the tropical year—also called the "solar year" or the "calendar year" of 365.2422 mean solar days. To fit a number of full days, we need 5,000 solar years, or 1,826,211 days!

Anything less won't do. And the sidereal year of 365.2564 days is not much better. It takes 2,500 of these years representing 913,141 days. The gears of the computer would have to be too big to be practical. But the Sothic year of the ancient Egyptians fits like a glove for a small mechanical computer. It has 365.25 days, so we need only a gear ratio of 4:1 to obtain whole numbers of days and years. Every four years of this Sirius, or Sothic, calendar will give an exact number of days. The gears are small and manageable. This simple and practical year of the Egyptian priests makes many complicated astronomical cycles equally simple, an advantage which modern astronomers with their ingrained traditions have so far ignored. Use of the Sothic-year cycle makes it easy to calculate all periods of revolution of all planets, and all conjunctions, as well as all phases of the moon.

The second important condition for a successful construction of an astronomical calculator with gears is to find a simple relationship between the cycles in full, whole days. The Mayan calendar almost made it. So did the Sumerian calendar, which was based on the Saros cycle of eighteen tropical years. The Greeks used a calendar based on the Metonic cycle of nineteen tropical years, and this system has no practical value for a gear computer either, which proves that the Greeks were not so great mathematicians after all and that whoever constructed the marvel of Antikythera was a much stronger mind.

We are left with the ancient Egyptian calendar. It is the only one that fulfills all the requirements, and it is the basis for the Rhodes calculator. The seemingly complicated Egyptian calendar, based on Sirius, the sun, and also the moon, actually works like a charm. Every four years represent exactly 1,461 days which in turn represent 49.474 synodical moon months. This last number has to be multiplied only 19 times to give a number of whole days—27,759—equal to 940 months, or 76 Sothic years, which is the cycle of the Rhodes calculator!

It seems to me that the mechanism found on the Roman galley was a small, reduced model of a much more complicated and refined machine that the Egyptian priests used to calculate all the planetary movements in the solar system and more. But that calculator has not been found yet.

When men decide to make a really serious effort to explore the

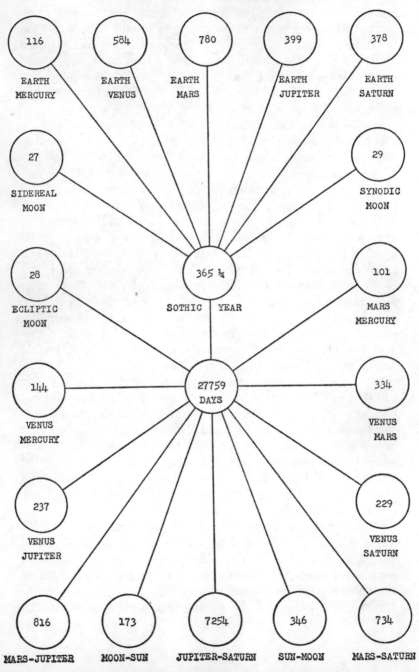

THE RHODES CALCULATOR

FIXED TYPE WITH 18 ASTRONOMICAL CYCLES

ground under and around the pyramids near Cairo we will probably find it. We know that, as a rule, all the other pyramids
stand on top of underground systems of passages and temples,
sometimes whole subterranean villages, and it would be very
surprising if the Great Pyramid of Cheops didn't follow the rule.
We are bound to find those hidden chambers some day, and
once we find them, we will have evidence that it was astronauts
from space who elevated us to our present pedestal.

Most of the ancient civilizations used the Sothic year to calculate the ages of mankind and of the world in fantastically high
numbers. The Hindus estimated man was 4.32 million years old
and the earth 4.32 billion. The Mayas arrived at far greater numbers. But the Sothic year is the basis of all great cycles known by
either Mayas, Hindus, Sumerians, Egyptians, Greeks, or others
that we know of. Aside from the cyclic relationships that were
built in the Rhodes calculator, the Egyptians also used others, all
based on Sothis-Sirius, who for them was the "good God who
makes all things green grow." One of these regular repetitions
came every 1,460 Sothic years, or 1,461 civil years of 365 days
each. Then both these years coincided with each other on July
19, the day when the Nile starts to rise, as the Egyptians
believed, by the command of the Sothis, the Dog Star. These
long Sothic cycles were documented by Egyptian astronomers as
having occurred on July 19 in the years 1320 B.C., 2780 B.C., 4240
B.C. and 5700 B.C. The Sothic cycles are bringing us far in the
past indeed.

The Rhodes calculator and the recently so popular Piri Reis
maps that show the ancients knew the Antarctic continent are
both copies of much older originals. And since neither bronze
nor parchment are very durable materials, the survival as well as
the rediscovery of these items do make one wonder if there
wasn't some of what I describe as benevolent intervention of the

This astronomical calculator, discovered in 1900 at the bottom of the
Aegean Sea west of Crete and probably built more than 2,000 years
ago, was based on a long-forgotten Egyptian cycle of 27,759 days, or
76 Sothic years of 365¼ days each. By means of gear trains, this
cycle was divided into eighteen different astronomical cycles. The cycles indicated here are the most accurate that could be obtained with
a minimum of gear trains.

gods involved in the findings. The fact is that only stone does not change over eons. Under favorable conditions, in places like the Dead Sea region, some documents can survive a few thousand years, but not ten or twelve thousand. This is why we will never find the originals of the maps that the Turkish admiral and cartographer Reis copied in the fifteenth century and we will never see the original model of the Rhodes calculator.

However, the existence of the copies is enough to make us understand that some of man's highest achievements date back to the dawn of time and that the Rhodes calculator is a link in a chain that leads back to grand civilizations of an unknown past. There is a message for humanity in this ancient machine that I cannot decipher and even makes me suspect we are still not sufficiently developed to grasp its true meaning. This is a fact that annoys and disquiets me, and yet there are in this world some even more disturbing findings.

I'm talking about recent findings in all parts of the world of perfectly machined metal parts that were buried in strata of coal or rock hundreds of feet under ground and millions of years old. Cubes, spheres, and cylinders of perfect geometrical form have been dug up from such strata and nobody yet has been able to explain these findings without admitting the possibility that indeed our most ancient forefathers were capable of making precision gears out of thin sheets of bronze and to assemble them into clocks useful for astronomers, mankind's oldest scientists.

It is very difficult for me to respect those scientists whose minds seem permanently closed. After all, most of today's scientific equipment and techniques just did not exist a short one hundred years ago, when Paris and London academies of science thought they knew everything already and wanted to ignore every discovery that disturbed their theories. If in the last century we have achieved as much progress as we actually have, it has happened only thanks to independent, unprejudiced minds outside the establishment.

We were told that machines heavier than air would never fly, that the sound barrier and air friction would kill pilots and melt the planes and that rockets would never be able to overcome earth's gravity. Man will never walk on the moon, said most scientists not so long ago.

Well, man did, and I was part of the team that made it possible. To tell you the truth, before the landing module from Apollo 11 landed on the moon we were not so sure either. The monumental project needed constant changes and inventions that were not even conceived of at the start. We went along improvising and improving and making impossible things possible. Apollo was constructed and built in a few short years by several thousand capable engineers. There were real geniuses among them, and they came from all nations.

We all recognized one fact—that in our native countries, be it England, France, Germany, Japan, or China, we would never have had a chance to prove our true potential. It was the free and untrammeled state of mind that made the moon shot possible, and, naturally, the unlimited access to means and material to make every new concept or idea work. All that was attainable only in the United States and nowhere else. The gods themselves know that I am not always a proud American, as I am not every day proud of my French origin. But I am proud to have been born and educated in France and proud to be an American by adoption and profession.

I want to say in conclusion of this chapter that the freedom of the unbiased mind has to be applied also to the recognition that probably nothing of what we invent now has not been invented and reinvented thousands upon thousands of years ago. Civilizations come and go, often without leaving a trace. Sometimes a remnant of the past is left behind to make us at least suspect that man was more intelligent and advanced in an earlier civilization that disappeared. The Rhodes calculator is such a remnant of the unrecognized past that miraculously escaped the destruction of a very ancient civilization.

CHAPTER 6

The Kings of the Sea

UNTIL A FEW YEARS ago the general belief was that it was impossible to navigate oceans without compass, sextant, chronometer, or sighting land. The question how our ancestors then managed to reach distant lands across open seas was unanswered. We know primitive compasses and sextants existed, but there were no chronometers deemed necessary to determine the longitude. The first such transportable clock movement was fabricated in France around 1525, but the first ship chronometer dates back only to 1736 when, after eight years of tedious work, John Harrison of England completed his masterpiece.

The official scientific answer to the riddle of how men could navigate was simple. We were told our forefathers never let land out of sight and navigated along the coasts only. This we were taught in school and this we were supposed to believe even though it was only one of the many blunders that our learned academicians were guilty of. Another fallacy in the same category was the tale that the American continent was populated by migrants who came from Asia over the frozen Bering Strait, even though archaeological and ethnological discoveries demonstrate conclusively that men did know how to navigate tens of thousands of years ago and had no need to wait from one ice age to the next to make the crossing to Alaska. In fact, they didn't hesitate to cross the ocean on rafts or on ships.

Still, how exactly did they do it? By what means were they able to determine in open sea the two co-ordinates of longitude and latitude in order to know where they were and where to go? The theory that all ancient ocean crossings were accidents caused by wind or current could not be true. Too many legends report of planned voyages and of heroes who visited distant lands and returned to tell about their adventures.

When ancient Roman coins were found in Venezuela, Sumerian mining colonies discovered in Peru and Bolivia, and Hindu cotton and jute plantations traced in Mexico, I began wondering and searching again for the answer to the riddle of ancient navigation and now I believe that I have found the answer. Instead of chronometers, they used sunset and moonrise tables that were skillfully calculated for every day of the year in the case of long voyages and for many years to come. Thus at any time a navigator of a ship on open sea could determine his location by comparing the actual times of sunset and moonrise to those charted for the same day for his home port.

Since latitude is easily determined by an astrolabe or primitive sextant, the difficult part was the determination of the exact time span between the moments when the sun disappeared and the moon showed up. It was done by a battery of hourglasses set to measure a fraction of a minute. Let me explain with an example from our recent past what the sunset-moonrise timing has to do with the geographical longitude that has to be found.

All astronomical phenomena of short duration, like an eclipse, are never seen simultaneously at different points of the globe. So, for instance, during the total solar eclipse of June 30, 1973, that lasted up to 7 minutes 3 seconds, the shadow of the moon was running eastward over our earth in a narrow band 240 km wide at a speed of 2,150 km per hour. In order to observe the eclipse a little longer, seven astronomers from England, France, Scotland, and the United States used a supersonic Concorde equipped with all necessary instruments to fly east at an altitude of 17,-000 m (56,000 ft) so they could watch the eclipse for 84 minutes. To enable them to do this, the plane naturally had to move with the same speed as the shadow of the eclipse—2,150 km ph—which it did easily. (This eclipse came exactly nineteen years after the mysterious one of June 30, 1954, that we will discuss later on in this book.)

The period of totality of the June 1973 eclipse varied one full minute for every 36 km at the same latitude. If the eclipse took place over point A at noon, seeing it in point B a full hour later would mean that the distance east from A to B, if both these points are on the same latitude, was exactly 2,160, or 60 times 36 kilometers. Now, eclipses are not a daily occurrence, so our ancestors had to find some other phenomenon of short duration that could be timed by simple means every day. Sunset and moonrise made possible for them to use the principle just explained and find more or less precisely how far away they had moved since they left home port or had passed some marker that was calculated for sunset and moonrise in their tables. Such astronomical tabulations written in cuneiform style have been found by the thousands on clay tablets in archaeological excavations in Mesopotamia. With the help of these timetables, ancient navigators could easily determine their longitude by using every 2 minutes of sunset-moonrise difference for 15 longitude degrees of travel since the start of the voyage. If, for instance, the trip had started in Alexandria going west and the local sunset-moonrise difference in the open sea was 54 minutes instead of 48 minutes for the same day in Alexandria, the ship had to be as far west as the Canary Islands, 45 degrees west of Alexandria. When at the same time the astrolabe reading indicated a latitude of 28 degrees, the captain would order the lookout on top of the mast and the helmsman to take extra precautions because these readings told him that his ship was in between the Canary Islands.

If all this sounds complicated to the uninitiated, believe me it is not. Such checks and comparisons were entirely within the capabilities of our ancestors who figured even much more complicated movements of celestial bodies, like the cycles of conjunctions of Jupiter and Saturn and the precession of the equinoxes.

The moon and the sun are exactly in line with our earth every 346.62 days. This period is called the lunar year, or ecliptic year, because during this time one eclipse of the sun can occur, followed by an eclipse of the moon 173.31 days later, when our planet passing between the sun and the moon throws its shadow on the latter. Whether or not these events will occur at all or whether there will be total or partial eclipses depends on complicated movements within the celestial vault that are well understood and present no problems to astronomers. I will skip the procedure of these calculations here because this book has too many numbers and ciphers already.

Astronomers who specialize in calculating eclipses have made up tables for thousands of years in the past and the future, showing the dates, hours, and zones of visibility for all eclipses all around the world. These modern tables are very useful to archaeologists and historians for checking the dates of certain past events described as having occurred during eclipses. For instance, it is one way to confirm that King Herod died on March 13, in the year 4 B.C., since historical documents mention a lunar eclipse on the day when he passed away.

Some eclipses have a history of their own. Such is the oldest recorded darkening of the sun, in China about 4,000 years ago on April 26, 2137 B.C. Two official astrologers of Emperor Chung Kang, who were paid mainly to predict eclipses so that the population could be told in advance not to panic, got stone drunk on rice wine on this day and forgot to give the warning. Neither could they, as the custom required, stand up to shoot arrows at the monster devouring the sun. So the two culprits, Ho and Hsi, were decapitated on the spot, and since that time Chinese astrologers drink nothing but water on days when eclipses are expected.

Another famous solar eclipse took place on a battlefield in Lydia where, on October 9, 583 B.C., the Medes and the Lydians after five years of war had lined up for the final attack at sunset. The sun rose in a blue sky and disappeared in a black shadow. The combatants laid their swords aside and promised each other never to fight again. To make sure that the promise would be kept, each king married the other's daughter. Peace was kept for several generations or as long as this historic eclipse was remembered.

The knowledge of precise dates for eclipses of the past has advantages for scientists who study the biblical events and try to rectify obvious errors. For example, we read in Amos 8: "I will make the Sun disappear at noon and I will cover the earth with shadows on a clear day." This is the perfect description of a solar eclipse, but most Bibles note 787 B.C. as the year when this event took place. Our tables show that this date is an error because the only solar eclipse around that time that was visible in Samaria, then the capital of Israel, happened on June 15, 763 B.C., or twenty-four years later than the Bible annotators tell us. Besides, when this time adjustment is applied to other dates of biblical events, these dates coincide perfectly with the dates given by Egyptians in their chronicles.

But let's return to navigation. We know now for certain that even before the chronometer was invented, the ancient mariners using lunisolar tables and hourglasses could, whenever the moon was visible, determine their longitude within one degree, or approximately 60 nautical miles, which is a very remarkable accuracy considering the errors later navigators report making even long after the chronometer had come into common usage.

In 1703 French mariner René Duguay-Trouin was leading his ships for nine days through thick fog along the Dutch coast and tried desperately to keep track of his longitude with hourglasses and pocket watches. When sun was sighted on the tenth day and readings of precise solar time made, the error of the sand hourglass timing was eleven hours and the difference that the pocket watches had accumulated was even greater.

The Solomon Islands were discovered by Spaniards in 1567 and carefully charted by solar sightings, but for two hundred years after nobody could find them, although this chain of islands stretches for over 1,500 miles in the Pacific. When by accident Solomon Islands were rediscovered in 1767, all maps of the Pacific had to be changed because the first entry had been false. The same thing happened to Pitcairn Island. Fletcher Christian, the chief of the mutinous crew of the British naval vessel *Bounty,* arrived there in 1789 and found that his refuge was off by several hundred miles from the spot where it was shown on the nautical maps. This was the reason why he decided to stay there, and he was proven right in his assumption that the British Admiralty, using its own erroneous maps, would not find him.

All these examples show that during the Christian era the great skill of navigation which was demonstrated by our distant ancestors slowly deteriorated. In the last couple of centuries all kinds of silly proposals were made how to improve navigation over wide oceans. None of them was so simple and efficient as the ancient moonrise tables. Some scientists proposed to measure simultaneously the angle between the moon and certain stars that is different at different points of the globe, but the precision needed for such measuring makes it impractical for small instruments aboard a ship. It was even proposed that a satellite of Jupiter be observed for calculation of longitude at sea, an operation that I certainly would not like to be in charge of, since Jupiter is above us only in daytime and no pair of binoculars usable aboard a ship will show its moons.

Another fanciful proposal without any practical merit was to anchor ships on each meridian and let them shoot colored flares every hour on the hour to indicate longitude to vessels passing by. But how do you measure exact distance over open water with the techniques that were at the disposal of seamen in the nineteenth century? And how do you anchor a ship in mid-Pacific? The well-known American writer of the last century Edward Everett Hale wrote a science-fiction story called "The Brick Moon," in which he came up with a brilliant idea, and established himself as the inventor of the navigation satellite, the backbone of modern navigation today. In Hale's book a man-made moon constructed of bricks was orbiting our globe with the precision of a pendulum, probably every ninety minutes. The time of passage of this satellite through the local meridian gave the exact longitude much as a passenger on a train that is exactly on time could tell where the train is just by looking at his watch and timetable, not out the window.

Today, the navigator of any ship lost in the thickest fog can easily determine his position within a few hundred feet, an achievement made possible by the three Transit satellites which the U. S. Navy in 1961 placed in polar orbits spaced 120 degrees apart around the equator and circling the earth every ninety minutes. Every parallel is crossed every thirty minutes, and because of the rotation of our globe, each following passage is 7½ degrees more in a westerly direction than the preceding one. After three passages of the satellites overhead, the ship's navigator can trace a very small triangle on his chart and knows that he is within these limits. The principle is very simple and only an hour is needed to do the job. A robot calculator using the Doppler–Fizeau effect usually does all the work. When the satellite passes overhead it emits a crystal-controlled frequency, a stable tone that changes as the whistle of a train changes when it passes by. The frequency of the tone received gets higher as the source moves toward you and drops as it moves away.

I know the Transit satellites very well indeed because the first three that were put in orbit were equipped with spherical spiral antennas that I invented and described in detail in *Aviation Week* on August 25, 1958. I also applied for a U.S. patent, but it was never issued to me for this invention because then the Navy would have been forced to pay me a compensation for the unauthorized use of this improvement in electronics. NASA also tried to use the same tactics with most inventors but had to change this course rapidly because it did not have quite the pull of the Navy and everyone who came up with a good invention kept it under wraps until a patent was issued to him which normally takes at least two full years. NASA could not wait that long and therefore decided to recognize the rights of the inventors.

Aside from the debatable methods that were used to obtain the elements of Transit satellites, this system is of great simplicity and unsurpassed precision. The calculator keeps working all the time and tells your position with an error margin of less than 100 feet. The only drawback is the price of this computer. Only the Navy, cruise ships, and the big oil tankers can afford it. The Air Force has long been peeved that it has to use the Navy system, and satellites and announcements have been made recently that a new and better system using more satellites and much lighter and more precise receivers will be soon put in operation by the Air Force. When that day arrives every electronics engineer will be able to construct less expensive equipment and make navigation even more precise and easier than it is already.

Now that we have seen how difficult it was to develop good navigation on earth, you can imagine how much more complicated it is in space. In fact, it is so difficult that up to now not a single space vehicle has been steered by its own navigation system. All depended on ground guidance. Tracking radar beams measure the distance and the angular co-ordinates of the launched space capsule from widely based stations. Ground computers establish the navigation data and corrections of trajectory, which are transmitted by radio. Even the astronauts in Apollo spacecraft who had a sextant and a telescope linked to an on-board computer did not make the slightest move without previous approval from the Houston Space Center. The crew was advised of all necessary maneuvers and the astronauts carried these orders out without questioning them.

But the day is not far away when interplanetary spacecraft will roam so far in space that they will be impossible to guide by radio or check by radar from earth. What then? Again, the same principle discovered by Austrian scientist Christian Doppler in 1842 and used for the first time by French physicist Armand Fizeau to measure the relative speed of stars will come to our aid. We will use the powerful radio signals transmitted by some emitting stars to guide our spaceships. These invisible radio stars are very powerful transmitters in space. Some keep sending continually in the 21-cm band, on the frequency of atomic hydrogen, 1,420 MHz. Three of these sources that have been chosen to guide our future spaceships are situated in the constellations of Cassiopeia, Sagittarius, and Taurus respectively. The distribution of these sources on the celestial vault is very favorable to the navigation of interplanetary spacecraft, which are always launched in a plane close to that of the ecliptic. Negative or positive Doppler frequencies obtained with the aid of a computer will guide our vehicles with great precision automatically, being compared all the time with the real course with the program and checked against the radio space markers of the stars. The radio source of Cassiopeia, which is the strongest one and always "visible" to radio telescopes at 40° N, is subject right now to intensive studies.

It is true that our forefathers did know electricity. Thousands-of-year-old electrical batteries have been found around Baghdad, Iraq, and a design for an electrostatic generator was discovered in Dendera, in Upper Egypt. But they did not use electronic gear to navigate around the world. Much simpler means were available. They used currents and winds that year after year flowed and blew in the same directions at the same time of the year. Just like the travelers of not so long ago who had to change from one steamship line to another to go to faraway places, so did our ancestors manage to cross the oceans by using the wind to pass from one current to another when the first one turned in a direction different from that where they wanted to go.

The global map of sea currents shows six main ocean currents, all of circular form, caused by the rotation of the earth. This is the Coriolis effect, and it is also what makes the water in your bathtub drain rotate clockwise in the northern hemisphere and counterclockwise in the southern.

With the help of the circular currents, it was always possible to come back home. The chance of a safe return was so good that regular transport lines probably were strung across the Atlantic and Pacific oceans.

The great North Atlantic current flows south along the coasts of Portugal and Mauretania to the Cape Verde Islands, where it turns westward to the Antilles, northwest between Puerto Rico and the Bahamas, then north to Newfoundland, across the North Atlantic and back to Portugal after skirting the shores of Brittany.

This current has a curious feature—it forms at its westernmost tip a smaller separate current of a circular form that encloses the Bermuda Triangle, where ships and planes disappear without trace, and the Sargasso Sea where migrating birds fly in circles for hours as if searching for an island that is there no more. This is the only place where the eels come for spawning, as if there were a river estuary there for them to ascend. The genetic memories of a distant past are demonstrating here most visibly the possibility that 12,000 years ago this part of the Atlantic could have been the sunken continent of Atlantis.

The South Atlantic current starts at the Cape of Good Hope, flows up along the West African coast as far north as Gabon, then crosses the Atlantic at its narrowest from east to west till it reaches Natal in Brazil, and descends in southerly direction to Buenos Aires, where it turns back east to the Cape of Good Hope.

Both these currents played very important roles in the past. After circumnavigating Africa, Hindu and Sumerian sailors used the South Atlantic current to go to the estuary of the Amazon, the Antilles, or the Gulf of Mexico, and if the search for traces

WINDS ⟹
CURRENTS →

CIRCULAR NAVIGATION ROUTES

USING WIND AND CURRENTS

This map shows how our ancestors could have crossed wide oceans without sextant, compass, or chronometer, using only winds and currents that would bring them back home a few years later. They could determine their latitude from the height of the polar star and their longitude from the relative motions of the sun and moon.

they left behind continues successfully, we will eventually have a map of all their incredible voyages.

The current of the North Pacific moves south along the coasts of California and Mexico, turns west at Acapulco, crosses the Pacific at its widest, passing south of Hawaii, and arrives at the Philippines, where it starts flowing north till it reaches Japan, turns east, and comes back to California. This current must have played an important role in the migration of the Asiatic races who came to America between ice ages, when the passage over Bering Strait was not frozen solid.

The South Pacific current moves north along the coast of Chile up to the northern part of Peru, then turns west and traverses the Pacific north of Tahiti and south of New Caledonia and the Hebrides. It skirts the east coast of Australia, hooks to the north and then twists south to evade New Zealand before returning to Chile by way of Easter Island and the Juan Fernandez island group off Chile. This current played a decisive part in the migration of Polynesian people to South America or vice versa. The only thing that we have to find out is who brought civilization to whom. In my opinion, the Polynesians are much more civilized than the Indians of South America, but that does not prove a thing, because I have been off the mark in my judgment many times.

The north current of the Indian Ocean starts from the east coast of Africa at the latitude of Zanzibar and flows north up to the estuary of the Indus River in Pakistan, then turns southeast to Ceylon, reverts in a northerly direction up to the River Ganges in the Bay of Bengal, flows south to Sumatra, in Indonesia, where it takes a western direction and flows back to Zanzibar by way of the Diego Garcia and gave passage to Egyptians from the Gulf of Aden and Sumerians or Hindus from the Gulf of Oman, and, after a cruise along the Sunda Isles, brought them back to Africa, the Mozambique Channel and the current of Agulhas that led them to the South Atlantic current for a passage to the Amazon, the Antilles or Mexico.

The southern current of the Indian Ocean has not been sufficiently explored. We know that it runs south along the coast of Madagascar, turns east at the latitude of Cape of Good Hope and crosses the most desolate ocean of the world, passing the islands of New Amsterdam and St. Paul, to arrive at the West Australian coast, where it changes direction and returns to Madagascar, flowing north of the islands of Réunion and Mauritius. We do not know the history or prehistory of this current, which probably also had importance in the very distant past when the continent of Antarctica was not ice covered and could have been the cradle of an advanced civilization.

In all three oceans there is an equatorial countercurrent be-

tween the big northerly and southerly circular currents. These
countercurrents are linear and they flow from west to east making it easier for navigators to change directions and pass from
one hemisphere to the other. It was these countercurrents that
enabled the Phoenicians, who, once through the Pillars of Hercules, or Strait of Gibraltar, sailed south to reach the Antilles or,

ACCESS ROUTES TO SOUTH AMERICAN METALS

FROM ATLANTIC TO AMAZON

This map of northern South America shows how ancient navigators
from the Mediterranean, after crossing the Atlantic with winds and
currents, could navigate up the Amazon, cross the Andes, and reach
the continent's gold, silver, copper, and tin mines. Moreover, the
whole Amazon basin could have been a huge inland sea many thousand years ago, making navigation much easier.

going a little farther south, the mouth of the Amazon River. Then, by sailing up the river, they could get close to the mines of Peru and Bolivia.

A map of these worldwide ocean currents looks very much like a big city's subway map. You have your different lines and the transfer stations from one line to another, and one of the busiest changing stations must have been the Canary Islands where all the traffic from and to the Mediterranean flowed by.

Once we understand how the ocean currents helped men to migrate, we can also understand why the monuments of Easter Island look so much like the ancient buildings of Tiahuanaco and the submerged ruins in the Bahamas; we can explain how Roman coins could be found in an old amphora on a beach in Venezuela and the 'remnants of Hindu plantation colonies, where cotton and jute were grown, on the east coast of Mexico. Sumerians and Phoenicians established mining towns in Peru and Bolivia to obtain copper and tin. To get there, these intrepid sailors had to navigate the Amazon for thousands of miles, and that is why mysterious inscriptions resembling the Phoenician alphabet have been found all along the banks of the world's biggest river.

In short, the use of the sea currents for navigation explains why all ancient civilizations seem to have so many things in common so that it looks as if all of them developed from one much older and much more advanced central civilization. The men of this central civilization were the Kings of the Sea and their art of masterful navigation and knowledge of stars and mathematics could very well have been gifts of astronauts who came from another world to educate and civilize them. Unfortunately, we may never know who these astronauts were or where they came from.

CHAPTER 7

The Signs of the Zodiac

TODAY ASTROLOGY has grown into such a huge and important sociological phenomenon that it takes courage to try to unravel its mysteries and auras. But we must attempt to determine once and for all whether astrology is an exact science like astronomy and mathematics or just a lot of humbug.

Quite a few people before me have already tried to do it. But they could not come to clear conclusions because they started with the intention to demonstrate the validity of their preconceived concepts. Some even went as far as to fabricate their evidence.

As for myself, astrology, like most other things in my life, came to my serious attention by accident. I am supposed to be a man of science, but I love many other activities, like diving for old gold doubloons off the Florida Keys or exploring the history of science. The latter activity focused my attention on astrology which, maybe, is not a science at all, but without which we never would have had astronomy, since after all it was the ancient astrologers who, during many thousands of years, accumulated their observations about the positions and movements of the heavenly bodies and tried to relate them to human or terrestrial events. And considering the very primitive means at their disposal, these men left behind incredibly precise records that can be easily matched with the best modern astronomical tables.

If astrology is a science, it is a very complicated one. It intertwines the objective information about the movements of the celestial bodies with the subjective projections of supposed influences that these configurations of stars will have in the lives of men and human destiny on earth. But the foundations for such speculations are very shaky.

First of all, astrologers have not up to this day figured out which is the most important moment when the stars cast their spell—is it the moment of birth or the moment of conception? Similarly, they have no final and clear definition of what is meant by an astrological conjunction of two planets. Is it the moment when they are at the same point in longitude as calculated by their cycles, which we will call the "theoretical conjunction," or is it the geocentric conjunction when we see it from the earth, or, finally, is it the heliocentric conjunction, the instant when these planets are in line with the sun?

On top of that, the second case of astrological planet conjunctions, the geocentric one, is totally confusing, because over a period of six months the variable angular velocities of Jupiter, Saturn, and earth can create as many as three such conjunctions and nobody can decide which is the right one.

The most famous of these triple conjunctions happened in 7 B.C., the year when Christ was born, in the sign of Pisces. If we can believe the latest tables of planetary conjunctions established by our best computers in 1962—and who else can we trust?— three different alignments in the same area of the skies took place that year between Jupiter and Saturn: first on May 14, lasting to June 3, with a maximum on May 24; the second on October 1, lasting to October 21, with a maximum on October 11; and the third on December 5, lasting to December 15, with a maximum on December 10.

This triple conjunction between the two planets so excited the astrologers of that time that the legend about the star of Bethlehem was born and with it the beginning of a new era in human history.

Triple conjunctions are very rare and seem to come only once every 973 years. The first one of our era arrived in A.D. 967 in the sign of Aries, on June 5, October 13, and December 12. Again in 1940, in the sign of Taurus, we had triple conjunctions on July

CAPRICORN · SAGITTARIUS · SCORPIO · AQUARIUS · LIBRA · PISCES · VIRGO · TAURUS · LEO · GEMINI · CANCER

AUTUMNAL EQUINOX · WINTER SOLSTICE · SUMMER SOLSTICE · SPRING EQUINOX

ARMENIA · CAUCASUS · AZERBAIJAN · TURKISTAN · PALESTINE · PERSIA · EGYPT · INDIA · NUBIA · ETHIOPIA · HADRAMAUT · YEMEN

This map of the Sumerian civilization shows the twelve countries around Sumer as well as the corresponding zodiac signs and constellations in 9700 B.C. Apparently, the zodiac originally served as a road map as well as a sky map.

24, November 6, and December 26. There must have been some others, but so far I have not had the time to find them. At any rate, these three examples should be enough to show that astrology, be it a science or an art, is not easy to master and requires a certain intelligence. Before even trying to decide if astrology is an exact science or a sham, which in itself is a delicate question, we should study a little the very basis of our modern astrology as transferred to us by the Chaldean Magis: the zodiac with its twelve mysterious signs.

Since the dawn of time, men must have noticed that certain stars hanging in the vault of the sky seemed to disappear behind the sun and that each return of the yearly seasons brought these stars back. This is how they must have realized pretty soon that the stars were immobile and the sun was traveling around and that the same path, only slower, was followed by the planets. In such a way, certain characteristic groups of stars were chosen to indicate every season of the year. The whole ring of constellations was given the name "zodiac," or circle of animals, because of all the animals our ancestors seemed to recognize in these star groups.

Depending on the region and the way they counted their sheep, goats, or cattle, our ancestors divided the band of the zodiac into eight, ten, twelve, or thirteen parts. One division was as good as the other because the constellations are not evenly distributed at equal intervals. The Chaldeans, like the Sumerians before them, had divided the band of stars into twelve parts because they counted everything by 12 or by 60. Actually, it is better to divide the zodiac into thirteen parts, since it is easier then to give each segment one characteristic constellation without gaps or overlap.

It is quite easy to design, with groups of the brightest stars in the zodiac, thirteen different triangles that have dissimilar forms and orientations and whose centers are evenly spaced about 28 degrees from each other all around the great highway of the ce-

This illustration shows a new zodiac made of thirteen equally spaced triangles and 39 corresponding stars. This is much more logical than our present Babylonian zodiac with twelve unevenly spaced constellations, some above and some below the ecliptic, which does not seem to make sense.

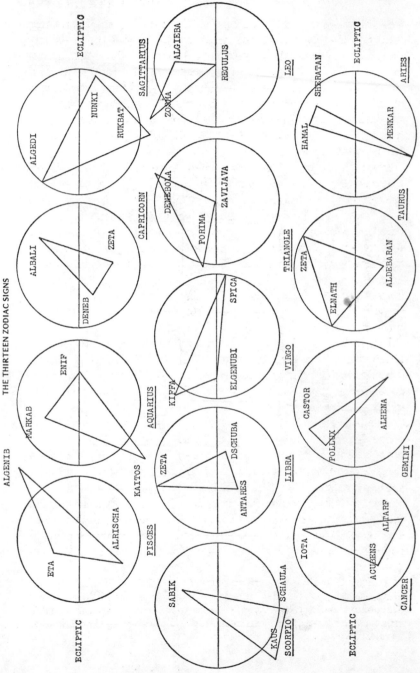

THE THIRTEEN ZODIAC SIGNS

PRESENT POSITION OF THE THIRTEEN ZODIAC SIGNS

ON THE ECLIPTIC AND IN THE SOLAR YEAR

lestial vault. Again, we have here the same magic number, 28, or 4 times 7, that we find all over the world, as in the 28 parts of the Maltese cross of the Aegean, the 28 sectors of the Medicine Wheel of Wyoming, or the 28 inches of the cubit of Giza, Tiahuanaco, and Cuenca.

Thirteen was a sacred number for the Mayas, and I believe they divided the zodiac in thirteen parts, even though so far I have not been able to prove it. The Mayan calendar consisted of 13 baktuns of 20 katuns each, representing 260 conjunctions of Jupiter and Saturn.

Some modern astrologers have already begun to use thirteen signs of the zodiac. Generally they place a new sign between Scorpio and Sagittarius, but it seems more logical to me to insert a new sign between Leo and Virgo. More available space is found there than after Scorpio, and so a new sign called "Triangle" could very conveniently be created by taking the bright star Denebola from the very tip of the lion's tail in Leo.

When I started to write this book I had no intention to devote a whole chapter to astrology. It seemed to be outside my subject matter for this account of my discoveries. If at all, only ancient astrology interested me, but my effort to discover as much as possible about the knowledge of our ancestors in all things astronomical forced me to become an expert in astrology. Doing all this research in a factual and precise manner, I could not help but notice the pitfalls and empty gaps of the old astrology, and this, in turn, made me seriously question the validity of the whole operation of our modern astrologers and their esoteric merchandise. Either the astrologers did not have the faintest idea themselves what it was that they were doing or they did not care what kind of product they were producing, as long as it sold. However, to make the public believe that high-grade value was offered, today's astrologers have given the old hoax a new twist. The ancient book of the Chaldean Magis is transferred to magnetic tape and from this data a computer can produce a

This illustration shows the present positions of the thirteen zodiac signs on the ecliptic and in the solar year. Each of them represents 28.09 days or 27.69 degrees. It also shows the relative positions of three major stars. Such a zodiac seems to have been used a long time ago by the Mayas who divided everything into thirteen and twenty.

nearly infinite number of different combinations, so that every client who pushes the buttons in a modern astrology establishment promptly receives a printout of his horoscope and goes home proudly convinced that for his good money he has received a tailor-made guide for his life based on all the mysterious secrets of the ancient wisdom and guaranteed to be true because a computer produced it. In reality all he has received is an absolutely valueless piece of paper. But what he does not know does not hurt him.

I had to ask myself what I would do if I had to reform astrology. Where would I start, considering all my knowledge of mathematics, physics, astronomy, and electronics and, above all, with my firm belief that stars do influence humanity. The answer was simple and there was only one—I would have to start from ground zero, from the very beginning, as was the case with the Apollo spacecraft and its communication system that fell in my hands and was my responsibility.

For me the universe with its billions of stars is a stage where comic and tragic plays are staged that represent each and every life here on earth. The actors are the sun, the moon, and the planets in perpetual motion, and depending on the positions or situations of these actors, the life of humans on earth can be paradise or hell. So I came to the conclusion that a new astrology should be created on a basis that would be fully valid for the next ten, twenty, or even more millenniums to come. To do this, we would first of all have to make an inventory of all visible stars within the zodiacal band (but not including constellations that change from one part of our globe to the other). In such a way we would create the permanent background, the stage setting for the main actors, and this background would remain the same for thousands of years.

Next we should concentrate on the 7 or 8 degrees of latitude on both sides of the ecliptic, which is the superhighway of the sky where the sun, the moon, and the planets move majestically and permanently. We should forget about the circumpolar stars for now, even though these will serve other purposes. After that, the stars in the band of the zodiac should be divided into small groups at equal intervals like the spokes of a wheel so that they would be easy to recognize and could be used as milestones to determine the exact positions of the sun, moon and planets at all times.

This concept of a new astrology first came to my mind in 1965 in Tahiti, where everything is so much simpler than anywhere else in this world. The western part of the island is ringed by a good road. It's about 80 miles long and it takes about three unhurried hours to drive its whole length before arriving back at the point where you started, like a planet in the zodiac. On Tahiti, except in Papeete, where the solid middle class lives, there are no streets and houses have no numbers. One lives at "kilometer 13" or "kilometer 17" and these indications are enough to find everybody. It was at the beach of Mooréa, an island 12 miles west of Tahiti, while I was contemplating the incredibly beautiful display of stars at night that I got the idea to reconstruct astrology, making the zodiac the dial of the big celestial clock and using the sun, the moon, and the planets as the hands for seconds, minutes, and hours.

The stars would have their permanent home, say, at 264° or 288° longitude, where anybody could find them at any time when he wants to, which is not quite possible today with even the astronomical zodiac, which displaces itself every year by 50 seconds of arc, and not possible at all with the astrological zodiac, which got stuck at the time of Babylon and has not moved since.

After I had decided to use the stars as mileposts, all that was left to be done was to make small groups of them at equal distances with easily recognizable configurations. Like any astrologer worth his salt, I used a computer and in no time at all I had the results. The best geometrical figure for grouping nearby stars is the triangle and the best solution to have them divided evenly is to use thirteen irregular triangles. At the same time, the computer, which never does things halfway, gave me all the celestial co-ordinates for each of the thirty-nine stars chosen to form these thirteen groups. The only thing I have not been able to find are the ancient names for all the stars in the thirteen new signs of the zodiac, but I managed to establish a sort of road map showing the triangles, their names, addresses, and the month when the sun rises in them in the morning.

I think that the new zodiac that I propose is one that was used by the Mayas, who counted by 13 and 26. In this "new" system each sign would change after every 28 days, 2 hours, 17 minutes, and 36 seconds, and these changes would take place on March 21, April 18, May 16, June 13, July 11, August 8, September 6, October 4, November 1, November 29, December 27, January 24, and February 21. The spring equinox would come as it does now —between the signs of Pisces and Aquarius, but the autumnal equinox would occur in the middle of a new sign—the Triangle.

The custom of considering the zodiac as a sort of a road map of the skies is well established, and it may indeed be true that the zodiac was first invented because of its usefulness as a road map. Do not laugh—such a thought is less ridiculous than it may seem at first blush. In our times, the spring equinox occurs on March 21, just about on the line between Pisces and Aquarius, while the autumnal equinox occurs on the line between Virgo and Leo. But 9,700 years ago these equinoxes occurred 135 degrees to the east, which means that spring arrived in the middle of the sign of Cancer and autumn in the middle of Capricorn, due to the precession of the equinoxes. We have excellent reasons to assume that the signs of the zodiac were invented at that time by the old Sumerians in Mesopotamia, who probably were refugees from some cataclysmic event, though we do not know who they were, where they came from, or when exactly they came to the valley of the Euphrates.

Now let us for a moment put ourselves in the shoes of the Sumerians who lived in their great city of Ur 9,700 years ago. We know they were great merchants, eager to sell their products to other people living in other highly developed centers of civilization like the valleys of the Nile, the Indus and the Tigris. Since the Sumerians counted by 12 and by 60, they probably divided the horizon around the city of Ur into twelve equal parts corresponding to the twelve regions of active commerce and exchange of materials that they wanted to cultivate with people living there. Just as the Fuller Brush Man and the Avon Lady cover the whole United States door to door and carry along their sample cases, so did the old Sumerians send their traveling salesmen in all directions. If you want to start north of Ur and go clockwise, Caucasus was north, Azerbaijan north-northeast, Turkestan east-northeast, Persia east, India east-southeast, Hadramaut south-

southeast, Yemen south, Ethiopia south-southwest, Nubia west-southwest, Egypt west, Palestine west-northwest, and Armenia north-northwest.

Now we have to remember that these traveling salesmen were most certainly illiterate. But they could count and were very good at memorizing their travel orders, which were given to them in the form of small tablets engraved with the signs of the zodiac. Gemini, the Twins, was the sign for Ethiopia; Virgo, the Virgin, for India; Pisces, the Fishes, for Palestine; Leo, the Lion, for Hadramaut; and so on. The stars of the constellations not only gave them the direction in which to lead their caravans of mules or camels but also indicated the right time for arriving at their destinations. The best time to arrive for business was when the sun rose in the morning within the given sign.

This system, however, has a flaw. The precession of the equinoxes changed the direction in which the salesmen were to travel. The spring equinox, which coincided with the sign of Cancer for Hadramaut 9,700 years ago was in the sign of Gemini for Ethiopia 7,500 years ago, and became the Taurus for Nubia 5,300 years ago. Either the signs or the destinations had to be changed to keep things in order, but we do not know if the one or the other correction was made or not. This question has never been answered, but we do know that today's astrologers use signs that do not correspond to the actual positions of the constellations in the zodiac, but do coincide approximately with the positions the stars held 2,500 years ago when the Chaldean astrologers did their fine work in Babylon. On the contrary, our modern astronomers use a zodiac where the spring equinox is determined for all times to fall on or close to March 21 when the sign of Pisces gives way to Aries, while the constellations where the sun rises at this date have slowly changed their places and have nothing to do any more with the positions of 9,700 years ago when the zodiac was probably invented.

This is the weakest of all points in our present-day astrology. It does not represent the actual astronomical positions of the stars today, it does not correspond to the signs when the zodiac was invented, but it approximately reflects the state of 2,500 years ago when the Jews were captives in Babylon. The zodiac of our present-day astrologers is the zodiac of the Bible, and this is why astrology is more religion than science. In a religion you are supposed to believe, not to ask questions or search for the truth, and today's modern astrology is not based, as it should be, on data derived from the stars or the planets, but on ingrained conventions that are interpreted differently by different astrologers at different moments.

The ancient Egyptians, who were great astronomers and in their day constructed the world's largest observatory, noticed that our sun moves slowly but surely among the stars by one degree every seventy-two years and therefore could not be trusted as a stable point of reference. This is why they chose the star Sirius instead and calculated their calendar and all their astronomical or astrological cycles by the apparent motions of the sun, moon, and planets in relation to the fixed position of Sirius. This is the most efficient and logical system ever devised and superior to any system used today.

But these arguments alone do not prove that astrology is just a hoax, as the majority of the scientific world assumes. It is nevertheless not only possible but most probable that modern astrology is based on faulty or totally false assumptions, even though it is true that the influence of the sun, the moon, and the planets do have a part in everything that happens on our planet as has been proven in hundreds of scientific experiments. Which reminds us once more that our ancestors, who grasped this tens of thousands of years ago, were not quite as dumb as is generally thought and that indeed this knowledge, too, was given to them long ago by the same astronauts who brought about the sudden leap forward in our evolution.

Since it is evident that stars influence mankind, it is not only quite possible but very probable that they also influence each individual and that astrology could be made into an exact science if all the correlations of cause and effect could be determined scientifically, precisely and correctly. Considering the fantastic possibilities that have been given us by the electronic brain and the magnetic memory, a rational reorganization of astrology would not require too much time.

All of us have our good and bad periods. Sometimes we can work twelve hours a day and not feel tired while on other days we have no wish to exert ourselves at all. Also, we all know how intelligent we can be when feeling good and what stupid mistakes we make when we're not in our best form. There are periods when nothing works out no matter how hard we try. Most certainly this is so in my own life. The trouble is, I never know if at any given moment I am in my good or my bad period.

By way of observation, I have found out that these changing periods are cyclic and regular but as yet I have not found the governing pattern. It is very likely that these fluctuations follow some astronomical cycle like the conjunction of planets. Besides, we have already proven scientifically the influence that planets, namely Jupiter and Saturn, have on space communications. This is why I do not dare to say that astrology is all one big hoax. Maybe all it needs is a new reconstruction of the basic concepts and tenets from the ground up.

I sincerely believe that stars can influence my life, even though I still do not understand the mysterious rules that govern these influences. That, however, does not mean that I can believe in astrology as it is practiced today.

Recently published books about astrology have brought to my attention many interesting astronomical cycles. The works of Louis MacNeice and Serge Hutin contain numbers that correspond to calculations I have made with the Nineveh Constant, and the results are precise to the fourth decimal point. In my opinion, there is also a correlation that could be explained by influence of the stars between the Russian and American space programs. Both started suddenly at the same time, and in this period the world was flooded by books and publications all pointing in the same direction, namely, that we are not the first astronauts and that there have been visitors from space long before we first heard of Sputnik or Apollo.

It could be possible to believe that our Fathers in Heaven knew long ago that this day of liberation from our gravity field would come and that our exploration of space would start. If, as the Arab adage says, all is written down that has to come, it is not surprising that we are now offered the insight to understand our true nature as the sons and daughters of our ancestors who came from outer space.

CHAPTER 8

The Polar Mysteries

THE UNITS OUR ANCESTORS used for measurements never had any particular fascination for me, but I have always been attracted by ancient coins—the pieces of gold, silver, and electrum that were in circulation thousands of years ago. However, since all coins are also units of weight and weight is derived from units of volume, which in turn is derived from units of length, I got curious enough one day to find out why some particular coins were made of a certain weight of gold while others represented a different weight in silver. While working on these problems, I did not realize exactly what I was actually trying to discover, but just kept going on.

To do my work right, I had first to make a list of all the coins that had been in circulation since the time of King Croesus, who is considered to be the inventor of money. He ruled Lydia, an ancient Aegean country of Asia Minor, from 560 to 546 B.C. and was defeated and killed by the Persians under Cyrus who wanted his riches. Croesus minted the first coins from nuggets of electrum, natural alloy of gold and silver that could be found in the Pactolus River flowing by Sardis, the capital city of Lydia. These electrum coins are now almost 2,600 years old.

There might have been some more ancient coins, but so far none have been found. Legends tell us that 12,000 years ago in Atlantis coins were made of orichalch, a metal lighter in color and weight than gold, probably some alloy of copper and aluminum like the aluminum-bronze coins of small denominations that are used in France today. These aluminum-bronze coins oxidize easily, and this is probably why none of the Atlantis lightweight money has ever been found. It must have disintegrated long ago without leaving a trace. However, we still have a few electrum coins from King Croesus.

After I had compiled my list of most ancient coins known to numismatists and archaeologists, I had to make up another one for all measurement units of antiquity, translating these various units into feet and cubic feet. It took some time to get all this done but it was time well spent. Then I started to compare the two lists and try to find the feet whose cubes represented the weight of a round number of coins.

In most cases, quite naturally, the weight of the coin divided neatly into the local unit of weight for the corresponding country and the time in history when this money was in use, but there were quite a few surprising exceptions. In some instances, relationships showed up between vastly separated geographical locations and even greater differences in time. Coins of exactly the same weight had been found in geographical locations thousands of miles apart and in different cultures separated by thousands of years.

This is where my interest became really aroused and my work became exciting. Once more I was certain I had struck upon a mystery of the past worthy of exploration. But to make this clearer, let me first explain how our ancestors arrived at their basic units of measurement, now known as the inch, the hand, the foot, the cubit and the yard.

All units of measure in the distant past of our civilization had the same basic system in their foundations—all were determined from the true and exact dimensions of our planet earth. Incredible as this may sound to the uninitiated, our ancestors derived their feet and inches from the length of one degree of latitude or longitude. Quite naturally they used the longitude and latitude at which they lived and that explains why there were so many different feet and other units of measurement derived from the local degrees.

The length of 1 degree of latitude varies from 110,567 m at the equator to 111,700 m at the pole, while one degree of longitude varies from zero at the pole to 111,321 m at the equator. These two basic units of longitude or latitude were divided by an appropriate round number to obtain a measurement of length that approximated the average natural dimension of a human foot, finger, hand, or forearm. The Semites expressed their units in their usual system of counting by 10, while the Sumerians registered theirs by counting by 12 or by 60, and the Olmecs and the Mayas by counting by 20. But the basis for all these different calculations was the same—the true dimensions of earth.

The recognition of this fact does not, however, explain where our remote ancestors obtained such advanced scientific knowledge. Even the Greeks did not have it. Eratosthenes of Alexandria, the philosopher and mathematician, calculated the circumference of the earth 2,200 years ago and obtained a very passable value for it, but we know now that this happened by sheer luck. He made wrong calculations with wrong data but these mistakes were opposite in values and compensated each other. Even Pierre Méchain and Jean Delambre, the careful French surveyors who from 1792 to 1799 measured the distance from Barcelona in Spain to Dunkerque in France to obtain the base for the French metric system erred by a full 5 km over the length of their chosen meridian.

How come then that our forefathers back in the Stone Age had values so exact which we ourselves were only able to obtain after October 4, 1957, when the Soviet satellite Sputnik started to trace and measure the first orbits around the globe? We then obtained the exact measurements by observing the irregularities in the orbits of the first artificial satellites in order to calculate the true shape and dimensions of our globe. There is no better or easier way to do it. And yet our Stone Age ancestors had the same data. And this is why the measurement units of our ancestors become so utterly important for the scientific unraveling of the mysteries of our origin.

The numerous ancient drawings and sculptures found all around the globe showing astronautlike figures in helmets and space suits are pictorial testimonies from the farthest past that indeed visitors from outer space left their footprints here. But these paintings in caves and on cliffs are not scientific proofs of extraterrestrial visitations. But the precise knowledge of our fore-fathers of the length of 1 degree of longitude or latitude at any given point on the globe surely is proof, and so is the Constant of Nineveh, the cold, undeniable calculation in exact numbers that was used for thousands of years on both sides of the Atlantic by people who could never have obtained such information by themselves.

Our ancestors that came from outer space circled our globe and calculated the size of our earth from the time that it took them to orbit it at a given altitude and a given speed, as they also measured the irregularities of the sphere by the changes in their orbital velocity. This information was later—probably 64,800 years ago—given to the new generation of man. The weight of the ancient coins and the Nineveh Constant of the solar system are today two of our best scientific proofs that astro-nauts from space gave us their knowledge. But there are many others.

It is not at all difficult to understand how our ancestors calcu-lated their coin weight in gold and silver from the local dimen-sions of their longitude and latitude degrees. Here are four of the most striking examples:

At the average latitude of Egypt, the length of 1 degree of lon-gitude is 96,000 m. If we divide this number by 320,000, we ob-tain 1 ft of 0.3 m, or 30 cm, the unit used to build the Pyramid of Khafre. One cubic foot of this basic unit has a volume of 27,000 cu cm, or 27,000 gm of water. This is the weight of one Egyptian talent—27 kg. But the Egyptian way to write it is 60 sep of 450 gm each, or 600 deben of 45 gm, or again 6,000 kite of 4.5 gm. Besides, here is one of the oldest examples of use of the decimal system, if not the very oldest known today.

The median latitude in the region of the megalithic temples in England gives to 1 degree of longitude the average value of about 66,325 m. When that is divided by 240,000, we obtain 1 ft of 0.2764 m that was used to construct Stonehenge, and 1 cu ft of Stonehenge has the weight of 21,100 gm, or cu cm, of water. This weight divided by 2,500 gives a unit of 8.44 gm. No old coins of 8.44 gm each have been found in England, but the Mycenaean gold stater weighed exactly 8.44 gm.

Now, Mycenae in Greece is thousands of kilometers away

ANCIENT GOLD AND SILVER COINS

Weight in Grams	Name of the Coin	Country	Grams Unit Weight	Number of Coins
		GOLD COINS		
3.499	ECU	FRANCE	115,472	33,000
3.543	FLORIN	FIRENZA	28,700	8,100
3.605	DUCAT	VENICE	29,200	8,100
4.242	DINAR	ARABIA	28,000	6,600
4.548	SOLIDUS	ROMA	26,196	5,760
6.415	LOUIS	FRANCE	115,472	18,000
6.794	DOUBLOON	SPAIN	27,720	4,080
7.796	AUREUS	ROMA	26,196	3,360
7.975	SOVEREIGN	ENGLAND	31,104	3,900
8.333	SHEKEL	HEBREW	30,000	3,600
8.440	STATER	GREECE	21,100	2,500
8.600	PHILIP	MACEDONIA	25,800	3,000
16.723	EAGLE	U.S.A.	31,104	1,860
		SILVER COINS		
1.428	DENARIUS	GERMANY	34,265	24,000
1.460	PENNY	ENGLAND	31,104	21,300
1.693	DENARIUS	FRANCE	111,720	66,000
2.179	DUCAT	VENICE	29,200	13,400
3.397	REAL	SPAIN	27,720	8,160
3.898	DENARIUS	ROMA	26,196	6,720
4.220	TOURNOI	FRANCE	21,100	5,000
4.300	DRACHMA	GREECE	25,800	6,000
4.670	GROAT	ENGLAND	31,104	6,660
6.825	HEXA	BYZANTINE	25,800	3,780
14.545	SHEKEL	HEBREW	96,000	6,600
26.730	DOLLAR	U.S.A.	115,472	4,320
27.176	PESO	SPAIN	27,720	1,020

The weight of these coins was determined by dividing the unit weights, derived from the local cubic foot or cubit, by a certain round number which probably had a certain meaning. However, in some cases, a foot or cubit from another country was used. The most famous case is the Greek gold stater of 8.440 grams derived from the Celtic foot of 276.355 millimeters. Another strange case is that of the American silver dollar which seems to have been derived from an old French cubit of 486.960 millimeters. The Spanish silver peso of 27.176 grams worth eight reals is the famous piece-of-eight.

from Stonehenge, yet archaeologists have long been asking if there was any direct relation between this old Celtic site in England and ancient Greece. This because the outline of a Mycenaean dagger has been found engraved on a stone slab in Stonehenge. Now that we know that the Mycenaean stater has been derived from the Celtic foot of Stonehenge, which is much older than Mycenae, we may believe that perhaps it was the Celts who built Mycenae.

In Tiahuanaco, Bolivia, 1 degree of longitude is about 107,000 m. Divided by 360,000, this geodesic measure gives us a foot of 0.2972 m, which, with the cubit of 0.4458 m, is the construction unit of the Temple of Kalasasaya in Tiahuanaco. The Tiahuanaco cubic foot weighs 26,260 gm, the exact weight of the gold talent in Greece, which was also used all over the Eastern Mediterranean region, divided into 60 minas of 437.66 gm each or into 3,600 shekels of 7.29 gm each. But what is the connection between South America and the Mediterranean?

A degree of longitude at the latitude of the caves of Cuenca, in Ecuador, is nearly 111,230 m. Divided by 320,000, this gives a foot of 0.3476 m and 1 cu ft equals 42,000 gm of water. This weight could have been the base for several coins of our ancestors, but it is certainly the foundation of the gold tola in India, weighing 11.66 gm and still in use today in the Persian Gulf, where the Arab oil sheiks are paid for their oil in gold tolas freshly minted just for them. The Cuenca foot in my opinion could also be the ancestor of the Hindu foot of 0.2759 m whose cubic foot weighs 21,000 gm. This mystery is even more intriguing when we see it in the light of recent discoveries that the Hindus navigated all the way around Africa, across the Atlantic Ocean, and up the Amazon River to bring home copper and tin from mines in Peru and Bolivia.

No less surprising is the as-yet-unverified information from the Arabian Desert where very ancient pre-Islamic ruins have been found that seem to be built with a foot of 0.3037 m, a dimension that is new to us. Let's call it the foot of Baghdad. Some other sources recently indicate that a very old Arab map has been found, where the equator is divided not in the usual twenty-four or thirty-six parts but in forty-four equal arcs of 8.18 degrees each.

As archaeological findings go, the two discoveries would hardly seem to have anything in common. Yet if one uses a little bit of imagination and calculation, this first impression changes. The two bits of information could very well be pointing to a system of measurement used by ancient Arabs so very long ago that the Arabs themselves have forgotten it and that no archaeologist ever knew about.

Thousands of years ago before the decimal system became generally known, they didn't use the pi factor of 3.141593 to calculate the circumference of a circle. Instead, the much more convenient division 22/7 was employed because it was simpler. If the radius of a circle was 7 units, then the circumference was 44 same units. It is quite logical to use this same system to divide the equator into 44 units of 910,980 m each and to estimate the radius of our planet as 7 times 910,980 m, or 6,376,860 m, which is how the ancestors of the Arabs calculated the circumference of the globe at 40,083 km, instead of 40,075 km as we now measure it. Not bad at all, especially when one considers that instead of our precise figure of 6,378 km, they figured that the radius of our globe was 6,377 km.

When we divide 910,980 m by 3 million, we obtain a foot of 0.3036 m, nearly the same as the foot of the valley of Indus of 0.3018 m or the feet of the Egyptians or the Mayas that measured exactly 0.3 meters.

This new foot measure of Baghdad could very well have been the base for at least three monetary systems. One cubic foot of Baghdad would displace 28,000 cc of water and weigh 28 kg. Such a weight would equal 6.600 gold dinars of 4.24 gm each as used in Arab lands, or 9.600 dirhams of silver of 2.92 each in circulation all over North Africa, or even 2,600 gold or silver rupees of 10.77 gm each in India today.

It is not difficult to believe that our ancestors knew the approximate dimensions of our planet and used this information, clad in religious rites and rules, to express it in measures that corresponded to the human limbs. We can even accept the fact that the rotation of the earth's surface had been estimated at 1,000 Babylonian cubits of 0.4629 m per second or 100,000 Mycenaean feet of 0.2777 m per minute, fantastic as it may be. But when we have to recognize now that our forefathers knew the perimeter of the globe better than we knew it up to twenty years ago and that they used this exact knowledge in exactly the same way from continent to continent, such admission becomes very difficult unless we allow our skeptical minds to accept the theory of extraterrestrial visitors participating in the formation of our fate.

It seems certain now that further studies of weights and coins of the distant past will lead to the discovery of a central culture common to all mankind and stemming from the unknown place on our planet where the astronauts from outer space first landed about 65,000 years ago in order to foster a new race of earthlings.

One thing that can be said with certainty now is that all the measurement systems ever used, no matter when or where, share a common relation to the dimensions of our planet and therefore to the metric system. In its modern form that system was established only some 200 years ago in France. But, of course, the metric system was not invented by the French. Nor was it invented by the Egyptians who used it 5,000 years ago or by the Mayas who built their terraced pyramids in metric dimensions. The system must be even older than the Sumerian sexagesimal way of counting or the Mayan vigesimal numeration. It must have been developed by a civilization familiar with decimal counting, positional calculation, and the use of zero, a civilization which we have not yet found and probably never will find on the continents or islands known to us because it must be more than 100,000 years old and has probably been hidden in the depths of some ocean for tens of thousands of years.

According to the most recent theories, there were four original civilizations that appeared simultaneously at four equidistant points on earth in the Arctic, Indian, Atlantic and Pacific oceans. All of these points are now under water, but hundreds of thousands of years ago these were continents and they will rise again when our present continents in turn sink.

This theory is based on a very simple observation that everyone can make with an orange kept in a dry place. After a month or so the juice will have partially evaporated and the soft core will have shrunk more than the hard rind. The orange will have changed form from a sphere to a tetrahedron which has a higher surface area in relation to its volume than a sphere. Our earth has shrunk like an orange while its core cooled off and has formed four continents and four big oceans that keep moving all the time and travel from one geographical location to another very, very slowly in relation to the rotational axis of our planet. These global movements could be called the polar rounds and they make it difficult to calculate the correlations between different measurement systems in different countries of the world if these systems are many thousands of years old.

It is necessary to know the displacements of the poles to come up with the right results, because each local standard of measurement varies with time. This is why I am convinced that only a system of measurement that does not change with the polar rounds could survive the time, and this system could only be based upon the unchanging circumference of our globe, not the changing longitudes and latitudes. The metric system is like that, and it must be as old as humanity itself.

Not too long ago the geologists discovered that the hard outer crust of our earth floats on a molten mantle and that continents rest on separate tectonic plates. There are direct relations between the sliding of the plates and the changing of the polar ice caps, and what interests us here are the dates when these changes took place and their influence upon the lives of our ancestors. It appears that, in round figures, the poles remain stationary for periods of about 30,000 years, then move around for 6,000 years, then again stay put for 30,000 years, and so on.

Scientists have established that the last four rounds of the poles started 126,000 years ago when the North Pole installed itself in the territory of Yukon in Canada at 63° N and 135° W; then it went to the Greenland Sea at 72° N and 10° E about 84,000 years ago, moved from 54,000 till 48,000 years ago and settled in the middle of Hudson Bay at 60° N and 83° W; it rested there for 30,000 years; then wandered again from about 18,000 to about 12,000 years ago when it came to its present location. Simultaneously the South Pole went through similar gyrations but in the opposite direction. We have to note that its three previous locations were in their turn in the southern part of the Indian Ocean between Australia and the Antarctic but never on Antarctica itself. Only the last movement 12,000 years

THE LAST THREE DISPLACEMENTS OF THE POLES
FROM 90,000 TO 12,000 YEARS AGO

NORTH POLE

SOUTH POLE

ago brought the South Pole to the middle of the great icy continent of Antarctica.

At least half of Antarctica toward South America and the South Atlantic was ice free for 100,000 years, while Palmer Peninsula and Cape Horn that may not have then been separated from each other, enjoyed a fairly warm climate. There is no valid reason to doubt that during these periods of the last three polar rounds a very advanced civilization could have existed in this region and might have been the origin of all civilization and knowledge in astronomy, mathematics, metallurgy, and a variety of arts.

Much has been written about the polar rounds but very little has been said about the accompanying shift of the equator. The displacement of the tropical zones around the globe had certainly much more influence upon humans than the shift of the ice caps. Certainly climatic changes in the Temperate and Torrid zones have caused many more migrations and led to the destruction of many more civilizations than any changes in polar regions.

The polar rounds and the shift of the equator also explain why we have found traces of civilizations in regions of the earth that today seem unfit for human habitation. The jungles of Guatemala and Cambodia, the icy high plateaus of Tibet, or the deserts of Arabia were all quite different at different turns of the polar rounds, and this simple explanation solves many archaeological, ethnological, and geological mysteries.

If we consider where the equator was 90,000 years ago we discover that this line was very close to many famous archaeological sites like Hoggar in Algeria; Tibesti in Chad; the northern part of Egypt; Bahrein, in the Persian Gulf; Dilman, in Azerbaijan; Sumer, in Mesopotamia; the southern part of Persia; the Indus valley; Angkor, in Cambodia; Malekula, in the New Hebrides; Rapa, in Polynesia; Easter Island, in the South Pacific; Pisco Bay and the Nasca plateau in Peru; Tiahuanaco, in Bolivia; and the Amazon delta.

This illustration shows the positions and motions of the North Pole and South Pole at different times in the past. It shows in particular that, until 12,000 years ago, Antarctica had a much warmer climate and could have been the site of a long-forgotten advanced civilization.

Tracing the equator line of 54,000 years ago and starting again from Africa around the world we find that it touched the ruins of Zimbabwe, in Rhodesia; the anthropological sites of Java; the Nan Madol ruins of the island of Temuen in the Carolines; the Hawaiian Islands; the Galapagos Islands, in the Pacific; the caves of Cuenca, in Ecuador; and again the mouth of the Amazon. On the equator of 18,000 years ago we find the kingdom of the Queen of Sheba, in southwest Arabia; the Indus valley; Lhasa, in Tibet; Changsha, in China where a 2,000-year-old mummified princess was found; French Polynesia; and Easter Island. Naturally, not all old cultural sites are on these lines of the equator of the last 100,000 years. But it is significant that we find there the most mysterious ones like Angkor, Nan Madol, Tiahuanaco, Nasca, Cuenca, Machu Picchu and Easter Island.

There must have been a good reason why all these impressive civilizations established themselves around the equatorial zones of their period. Three reasons can be seen right away. First, there was the flight from ice ages that most probably in the distant past destroyed great parts of humanity more than once. The second reason is astronomical and nautical. If you stand on the equator, all stars are visible—Polaris, the polar star, and the Southern Cross too. It is the best place to study the movements of the stars, also the best place for navigation. All you do is observe the polar star for your latitude, and figure out the longitude by observing the time difference between the sunset in the west and moonrise in the east. The third reason is extraterrestrial. It is easier to handle a spaceship near the equator than in a polar region, just as it was with our landings on the moon.

No matter what all the reasons were, the zone between the tropics of Cancer and Capricorn, the borders of the tropical belt around our planet, has played the most important part in the development of civilization. During the ice ages the climate there was very pleasant, the sea level in the oceans much lower and all distances between islands and continents substantially shorter than now. Navigation was simpler because all centers of culture and commerce were on the same line and one could simply go with the sun to find them all. There can be no doubt any more that human civilization has lasted much longer than was previously thought. For instance, the latest radioactive carbon data collected from megalithic tombs in Brittany, Spain, and Wales show that these European remnants of ancient cultures are at least 2,000 years older than the pyramids of Egypt or the ziggurats of Mesopotamia.

But we still have to find out where it all began. What was the beginning of civilization? Was it the time when humans first started to communicate by sounds or gestures? Was it when humans made their first attempts to write or count? Or was it when they began toolmaking? Just recently the discovery was made that ancient iron ore mines in South Africa are 43,000 years old. And yet ancient records contain even older indications of culture. Egyptian priests once claimed that their ancestors had seen the sun rise twice where it set, which represented 40,000 years. Mayan documents in the archives of the Vatican state that their time counting started three long periods ago to give us a date almost 21,000 years ago. Unless I made a mistake in my calculations, the Nineveh Constant came into human possession 64,800 years ago, and we probably can't go wrong if we assume that indeed civilization began during the Cro-Magnon period 65,000 years ago.

The understanding of the polar rounds and of the wobbling equator will allow us some day to make the ultimate discovery in Antarctica, the most mysterious of all the continents. Antarctica wasn't visited (or perhaps revisited) until 1820, yet there are several very old maps that show Antarctica without a trace of ice, with rivers and mountains where today one finds nothing but glaciers. The two Piri Reis maps, dated 1513 and 1528, are copies of much older ones going back thousands of years, and as studies sponsored by the U. S. Navy Hydrographic Office have shown, these maps are utterly precise and in true scale. Even more interesting, they show many details that could only be found by survey, and yet these cartographic achievements must have been made at least 20,000 years ago.

This reminds one of the French writer, René Barjavel, who wrote a novel about an ancient civilization that was discovered under the mile-thick ice of the Antarctic continent. Why not? As far as I am concerned, it could very well happen that some day we will discover the Antarctic cultural sites just as we have found one after another the cities of Troy, Mycenae, Knossos, and Dilman. There is no reason why some day in the maybe not so distant future we could not find the sunken continent of Atlantis and the mysterious Land of Mu under thick sheets of ice or under the waves of an ocean.

CHAPTER 9

The Universal Calendar

THE SEARCH FOR A universal calendar that would enable all people all over the world to chart the past and map the future exactly and precisely has been going on since the most ancient times. Our ancestors did try repeatedly to find a time-counting system that would be independent of human events and happenings on earth, a calendar that would correlate simultaneous moments of time in one common system all around the globe.

It is hard to believe that still no such calendar exists. One of the most backward features of our modern age is our time-counting system, which was introduced during the Middle Ages by a Pope who believed that the sun circled the earth and began the counting of time from an event of uncertain date, the birth of a Messiah who may or may not have existed. That we use such a system when we have computers and travel in space seems beyond belief, but the worst fact is that *this outdated calendar* has three ways of counting time. There is our Christian Gregorian calendar (of Pope Gregory XIII). There is the astronomical calendar known mostly to astronomers. And then there is the calendar of mathematicians, who are the only ones to use it.

As an example, let's take the Gregorian date of March 21, seven years before the Christian era. For one using the astronomical calendar this would be March 21 of the year —60. The mathematician needing an expression that can be fed into a computer would in his turn translate that March 21 into the 286th day before the end of the year, the equivalent of 0.783 of one year, and write our date down as —6.783. Such an expression can be fed into a computer, it can be compared to any other positive or negative dates in Gregorian, Hebrew, or Moslem calendars, and it can indicate the time with fantastic precision of a few seconds, minutes, or hours, depending on the number of decimals used.

But such a system is neither easy or simple to use, nor very exact. It would be much simpler to count in whole days and in positive dates only, starting from an event very far in the past, preferably some exceptional astronomical event that took place at least 100,000 years ago, such as the alignment of all planets at the same point on the ecliptic that must have taken place at least once in the history of our solar system.

By pinpointing such a moment, we would establish a zero point for counting time and also a zero point in longitude—a starting line for all planetary movements. The whole world would then have a common chronological system enabling us to make all time computations childishly simple and precise.

I have tried to establish such a starting point in time and longitude for my own use but encountered some obstacles that seem to be at the present time impossible to overcome. The trouble is that the French astronomers on one side and the Russian and American astronomers on the other use different values for the same planetary revolutions and conjunctions, with considerable differences for Uranus, Neptune, and Pluto. The French data comes closest to the values obtained from the Constant of Nineveh for planetary revolutions, but any attempt to calculate the zero point in time and longitude from French data would be rejected automatically by the Russian and American astronomers. So I have given it up for the present, hoping that the time might come when uniform astronomical tables will be introduced globally.

The main problem is the impossibility to calculate precisely the past conjunctions of Mars, Jupiter, Saturn, Uranus, and Neptune. Here the Russian and American numbers are closer to those of the Nineveh Constant than the French data. The difference shows up in the third and fourth place after the decimal point only, but for calculations over very long periods of time the accrued error would be far too great for a precise calendar. Over a period of only 45,000 years the difference between the French and the American data would amount to as many as 3 years, and the same happens when we try to calculate the positions of these planets at that time. If I ask my French astronomers where the positions of the five exterior planets were in the year 3144 B.C. and if a conjunction took place, the answer will be, "No, there was no conjunction at this date according to the calculations of Urbain Leverrier and Gaillot." But my American colleagues will confirm a conjunction of Jupiter and Saturn in that year and another one of Uranus and Neptune 30 degrees further on the ecliptic. I would like to know who is right.

Still, establishment of a universal calendar would be possible if we used only the six planets closest to the sun, whose revolutions and times of conjunctions have been recorded and are known precisely. These movements have been recalculated recently for the past 4,500 years by two American astronomers, William Stahlman and Owen Gingerich using a modern computer. Their book gives the longitudes of these planets for every 10 days throughout this period, and it is easy to find the exact dates of all conjunctions of Jupiter and Saturn, the most regular among our planets. With this regularity in mind, it is not surprising for us to discover that several calendars before the Christian era were apparently based on these regular conjunctions of Jupiter and Saturn.

The Byzantine calendar starts on September 14, 5509 B.C. The Hebrew time reckoning begins on September 9, 3761 B.C. Both these years had a conjunction for Jupiter and Saturn. The same characteristic can be shown for the start year of the ancient Hindu time-counting, if it was the year 3104 B.C.

I have not checked all other calendars for this characteristic, but if we add to the above three, the Julian, Scandinavian, and Mayan calendars, we already have six that seem to have started in a year when there was a conjunction of Jupiter and Saturn. The Julian and Scandinavian calendars started in 4713 B.C. and the last cycle of the Mayan calendar began in 3144 B.C. This looks like more than a simple coincidence. The only calendar that escapes this rule of Jupiter and Saturn is the Egyptian calendar previously mentioned in this book as being based on the star

Sirius, or Sothis. The Sothic year of 365¼ days was used in ancient Egypt as a year of 365 days, repeated in cycles of 1,460 consecutive years. But even here it seems that the conjunctions of Jupiter and Saturn played a role. After an interval of 56 Sothic cycles, or 81,760 years, the start of the ancient Egyptian calendar coincides with a conjunction of the two planets. Again, we note that the number 56 has been mentioned several times before.

Besides the Sothic cycle, our ancestors had two methods at their disposal for calculating time, the solar-lunar system and the Jupiter-Saturn conjunctions. The first method was used for time periods rarely extending beyond 100 years. Ancient astrologers had noticed that the lunar month coincided with the solar year every 19 years, or after 235 lunar months, a period of time they called a "Metonic cycle." They also knew that the lunar month coincided with a solar eclipse every 18.03 years, or 18 years, 11 days after nineteen solar eclipses, or 223 lunar months, a period they named the "saros."

Using these two periods, the Metonic cycle and the saros, our ancestors formed longer time periods, like the Celtic Triangle used in Stonehenge that consisted of 2 Metonic cycles and 1 saros, equal to 56 years. The Mayas combined 2 Saroses and 3 Metonic cycles to make a period of 93 solar years. In my opinion, there must have been many other such combinations or solar-lunar cycles that have not been explored so far. Our ancestors must have noticed that after every 521 years, an eclipse of the sun took place during the same day of the year and in the same place in the zodiac. Also, that the saros and the Metonic cycle coincided after 235 saroses or 223 Metonic cycles and that 599 saroses represented exactly 10,800 years. This particular number 10,800 was a sacred one for all ancient cultures.

There can be little doubt that it took thousands of years of careful observations and notations to assemble this knowledge. Such important information had to be transmitted to future generations and not forgotten. This is why our ancestors built their calendars in stone. The most famous one is perhaps the megalithic temple of Stonehenge.

Its age is estimated to be about 4,000 years and its location is in the Salisbury Plain of southern Wiltshire, England. The geo-

CELTIC TRIANGLE

LUNAR MONTH

29.5306 Days

METON
19 Solar years
235 Lunar months

SAROS
19 Lunar years
223 lunar months

20,454 DAYS

SOLAR YEAR
365.2322 Days

LUNAR YEAR
346.6200 Days

56 Solar years - 59 Lunar years
Difference - 2.976 Days - 72 Hours

CELTIC CYCLE

MAYAN SQUARE

LUNAR MONTH

29.5306 Days

METON
19 Solar years
235 Lunar months

SAROS
19 Lunar years
223 lunar months

5 Lunar precessions

33,968 DAYS

SOLAR YEAR
365.2422 Days

LUNAR YEAR
346.6200 Days

93 Solar years

98 Lunar years

6793.4701 Days
LUNAR PRECESSION
Difference - 1.247 Day - 30 Hours

MAYAN CYCLE

This illustration shows that on opposite sides of the Atlantic, the Celtic builders of Stonehenge and the Mayan priests of Yucatán were using the same astronomical cycles and calculation techniques to measure long periods of time with lunar and solar eclipses.

graphical co-ordinates are 51.17° north latitude and 1.83° east longitude, giving a Celtic foot of 0.2764 m, which is the measurement used in the construction, as well as the corresponding cubit of 0.4146 m. All circles were traced with the ancient pi factor of 22/7—the three concentric rings formed by the partially destroyed outer ditch, two circles of Aubrey holes that held wooden pillars, and the ring of bluestone menhirs, now called the "Sarsen Circle."

The first ring has a diameter of 112 Celtic ft and a circumference of 352 Celtic ft, the second a diameter of 315 Celtic ft and a circumference of 990, while the third circle has a diameter of 385 Celtic ft and a circumference of 1,210 Celtic ft, equal to 334.40 m. These rings are in relatively good condition and can be measured precisely while three other circles, one made of bluestone and two of post holes, are more difficult to measure because of erosion but can be guessed as having had diameters of 84, 140, and 189 Celtic ft across and circumferences of 264, 440, and 594 ft, respectively. Inside the Sarsen Circle five arches indicated the setting and rising of the sun and the moon at different times of the year.

These five points of observation are placed like a horsehoe, with the open end facing the northeast and another a horseshoe inside, marked by the bluestone menhirs. The number of these stones, the intervals between the stones, and the wooden posts set in the holes gave a very high number of possible alignments that could be measured with great precision. When all this data is collected and fed in a computer to be compared with the positions of the most prominent stars in the past, we will be able to determine with precision the date when Stonehenge was built.

It should be noted that the circumferences of all circles measured in Celtic feet are exactly divisible by 22 and all diameters are divisible by 7—a proof of sound mathematics 4,000 years ago. Another testimony of the arithmetical ability of our Celtic ancestors is the interesting discrepancy that arises when 1 degree of the local longitude of Stonehenge is divided by 240,000. The result is a foot of shorter length than the foot used to construct the temple. This difference disappears when the latitude is changed by 2.35 degrees, which means, no doubt, that at the time Stonehenge was constructed the North Pole was 2.35 degrees nearer than now. Here again we have a good way to establish the true age of this megalithic temple. It could also mean that Stonehenge was part of a Celtic empire whose center was at the latitude of present-day Manchester and that the standard Celtic foot was calculated from the local longitude of the capital city of that time.

When was this time? Twenty alignments of Stonehenge have resulted in computer analyses of the positions of ten most prominent stars of 12,000 years ago, giving the exact rising and setting points for the stars Vega, Castor, Alcyone, Aldebaran, Altair, Betelgeuse, Rigel, Sirius, Antares, and Fomalhaut. All these stars describe in twenty-four hours a full circle around the North Pole, but only a part of these star circles are visible from Stonehenge, each marking two precise points at which the path of each star cuts the horizon. These twenty points are clearly marked in Stonehenge, earning very high marks in both mathematics and astronomy for our Celtic ancestors.

The solar and lunar alignments of Stonehenge are neither very interesting nor impressive, since identical alignments can be found all over the world. The temple itself is precisely built on the line of the summer solstice in the northern hemisphere—June 21. Other markers show the vernal and the autumnal equinoxes March 21 and September 22. There are also divisions of the circles showing the maximal north and south points of the lunar rising and setting. All these marks can be found with sufficient precision by anybody who wants to do it in a few years time.

What really impresses me about the mathematical and astronomical skill of these ancient priests of Stonehenge is the way they predicted lunar and solar eclipses. I would like to call it a program of advanced mathematical studies of the Stone Age, done with a few wooden poles and fifty-six holes. We all have long known that the Sumerians, the Egyptians, the Babylonians, and the Mayas were fantastic astronomers and mathematicians. But who expected such prowess from the Celts, the Hyperboreans of the Far North, rugged and unpolished ruffians? Yet since the recent discoveries that civilization invaded the Mediterranean basin from the north and after I studied the wonders of Stonehenge, I must admit that I am very proud of having Cel-

tic ancestors, the star-gazers and time-calculators of the deep
dark past.

The scientific skill and astronomical knowledge of Stonehenge
is rooted in the fifty-six Aubrey holes, in which at different dates
of the year were placed wooden poles of different height, giving
an astounding variety of precise alignments with the celestial
bodies. It made Stonehenge a huge, cleverly and skillfully exe-
cuted calculator. The time-counting cycle of these astronomers
4,000 years ago was the span of 20,454 days which, with a minimal error of only 72 hours, represented 56 solar years, 59 lunar
years, or 118 eclipses. This comprised 1 saro and 2 Metonic cycles I call the Celtic Triangle.

There is a relationship here to the Mayan solar-lunar cycle,
even though that was longer and more precise than the Celtic
Triangle. The Mayan cycle, that could be called the "Mayan
Square," comprised 33,968 days, giving, with an error of only 30
hours, 93 solar years or 98 lunar years, that is, 2 saros and 3
Metonic cycles. Since the Celts lived much farther north than the
Mayas and had much less favorable atmospheric conditions for
astronomical observations than the people near the equator
where the moon is nearly always overhead, I personally (my
prejudice granted) give the higher mark to the Celts. Also, I expect that much more will be discovered at Stonehenge than we
have seen so far. Nobody yet has taken the pains to try the markers for the five nearest planets, which must have been well
known to the astronomers of Stonehenge, or even for Uranus and
Neptune, probably familiar to them too. It could very well be
that in the patterns of Stonehenge some alignments are set to
indicate the conjunctions of Jupiter and Saturn at the time this
megalithic temple was built, and such a finding could help us
considerably in estimating its true age.

Stonehenge is so famous mainly because it is so easily accessi-
ble and so perfectly preserved. The megalithic temple of Avebury, about 20 miles north, must originally have been much
bigger than Stonehenge, as it was formed by 650 gigantic
menhirs encircling Silbury Hill. Yet the largest of all is the site of
Glastonbury, in Somerset, about 40 miles west of Stonehenge. It
is possible that this circle had a diameter of some 30 miles, but it

is so eroded and leveled with the ground that the exact size and configuration can no longer be readily established.

Some of these prehistoric temples of the Celts are not circular, but are formed by circles in combinations of different diameters. Woodhenge, situated next to Stonehenge, has the shape of an egg, also constructed in Celtic feet and with the pi factor of 22/7. It has an ovoid perimeter of 480 ft, or 132.67 m. In reality, Woodhenge temple is formed by six ovoid curves in perfect concentricity and mathematical relationship. Whoever constructed it was a master mathematician.

The British archaeologists and astronomers have adopted the megalithic yard as their unit of measurement to explore the prehistoric temples in England. This yard, of 0.829 m, equal also to 3 Celtic ft or 2 Celtic cubits, makes it difficult to analyze the true relationship of the Celtic civilization to other cultures of the past. Divided into megalithic yards, the diameters and circumferences of the circles do not comprise whole units and the prehistoric formula 22:7 is not apparent. But this relationship 22:7 is the base of nearly all prehistoric monuments—the Pyramid of Cheops, the temples of Teotihuacán, and others.

There also exists an American "Woodhenge," but the resemblance is in the proportion 22:7 only. The American site, the Cahokia Mounds, is constructed with the Tiahuanaco foot of 0.2972 m, which is quite surprising in itself. These prehistoric remains are in Illinois, near East St. Louis, on the east bank of the Mississippi River, and is only a part of an extensive maze of prehistoric temples, habitats, and truncated pyramids. The diameter of the Cahokia Mounds is 420 Tiahuanaco ft and its circumference is 1,320 ft, divided into 48 equal parts of 27½ ft each, separated by 48 equidistant poles. The observation point inside this circle is 5 ft off center in an easterly direction, from which point the vernal and the autumnal equinoxes could be observed over the top of a pole at sunrise. If one looks east, the fourth pole to the left indicated sunrise at the summer solstice and the fourth pole to the right, sunrise at the winter solstice. There certainly must be many other alignments built into this setup, but as far as I know, nobody has begun a serious exploration.

Prehistoric sites in the United States are not very popular. The Medicine Wheel of Wyoming is known because of its unique di-

vision into 28 parts similar to the 28 equal sectors of the Maltese
cross, but generally the exploration in the United States has
barely started. Most of these prehistoric sites are located in the
so called "Bible belt," where there is very little interest in pagan
temples of the past. However, this situation has recently begun
to change rapidly since even the farmers of the fertile Middle
West are coming to realize the value of their megalithic monuments and archaeological sites.

Before I close this chapter on Celtic temples I have to mention
a kind of configuration that is neither a circle, nor an ellipse, nor
an ovoid. It is formed by a combination of a half circle and a
half ellipse. The very little known and perfect example of this
form is a temple called "Long Meg and Her Daughters," which
is situated in the north of England along an ancient Roman wall
in Little Salkeld, Cumberland. This temple can also be measured by the Celtic foot and the ancient formula 22:7 of the circle.
The northern part of the monument is a half ellipse with a long
axis of 294 Celtic ft and a half short axis of 105 Celtic ft. The
southern part of the temple is constructed as a half circle, with a
147 Celtic ft radius. The north-south axis of the site is 30° off the
meridian, which could be a consequence of the displacement of
the terrestrial poles since the temple was built. The perimeter of
the Long Meg must have had originally 858 ft or 396 Celtic ft,
for the northern part and 462 Celtic ft for the southern. Translated into our present metric system, the surface of this site is
exactly 4,500 sq m, perhaps another of the recurring, as yet unsolved, mysteries of the metric system.

The temple is in such poor state that it is difficult to make out
which stones make what alignments. Too many are missing. It
seems quite clear, however, that this too was an astronomical site
built to measure time. But why the odd shape?

Some think that these configurations are the first signs of prehistoric geometry and that the different dimensions of this temple had the proportions of the sacred triangle of Sumer with
sides in the ratio of 3:4:5. This is not impossible, but it would
be very difficult to prove it. There could be another simpler explanation, easier to demonstrate conclusively, that will be
discussed in a later chapter of this book. The fact is that the elliptical apparent orbits of the sun and the moon and the appar-

ent diameters of the stars vary appreciably during the year. These variations of the apparent magnitude can be determined by sighting the object between two poles placed at different intervals in a circle and observed from the center at a constant distance. It can also be done at a variable distance from one of the centers of an ellipse, using poles spaced evenly on the ellipse. It is further possible that the elliptical orbits of the planets and the sun and the moon suggested some religious laws to our ancestors and that they found mystical meaning in the reproduction of such lines here on earth. It is even possible they had been told to do this long, long ago when our ancestors coming from outer space transmitted their wisdom to earthlings.

All the prehistoric temples, whatever their form and whether built in stone, wood, or heaps of dirt, had but one purpose—to measure time, long periods of time, extending over many generations. Oral transmittance was too vague to be trusted over millenniums. For a very long time, science ignored these temples and the Church destroyed many of them. Now these megalithic sites have become very popular, mostly because of the work done by a young English archaeologist, who proved that many of these sites are much older than any other known relic of human civilization, older than the pyramids of Egypt or the Tower of Babel. It seems that quite a few among these megalithic sites are as old as 12,000 years, the time when Atlantis allegedly disappeared in the ocean. It will take some time to prove it, but I do not doubt that it will be done. Right now, official science is beginning to recognize that some dolmens and menhirs in France, Brittany, Ireland, England, Spain, Portugal, and Morocco are 9,000 or 10,000 years old. And all these sites are clearly grouped around the eastern coasts of the Atlantic Ocean, like landing sites for an invading army of refugees.

The hypothesis of the survivors of the sunken Atlantis becomes more believable with every day spent in exploration. First there is the phenomenon of the Gaelic, Basque, Breton, or some Portuguese dialects that all resemble the dialect spoken in the Azores and particularly in the Canary Islands, once spoken by the Guanche people, which may be directly derived from the language spoken in Atlantis. Then there is the discovery of the strange blood groups. The Basques, people of unknown origin inhabiting the Pyrenees regions of both France and Spain, have a rare blood group pattern that is found only among other people speaking strange dialects and living near ancient menhirs and dolmens. Could this be the blood of the Atlantans or even the divine blood transmitted by the astronauts?

Above all there are the traditions that mark these people as groups of fearless seafarers inured to gales and tidal waves during a fabulous past. In order to navigate the oceans, this Atlantic race naturally needed the precise calculations of sunset and moonrise and the tables that showed them where they were during their voyages. To establish these tables, they needed observatories and they built them at Stonehenge, in England, at Carnac, in France, and elsewhere.

The possibility that survivors of the sunken Atlantis found refuge on the east Atlantic coasts and islands 12,000 years ago may also explain why the oldest among the world's sacred texts and legends mention dates much further in the past than the oldest Mediterranean civilizations or even the Egyptian pyramids. We could here examine some of the most distant dates and try to find if there is some correlation or even a similar method of reckoning among them.

Diogenes Laërtius, the Greek historian, mentions the year 49,214 before our era as the beginning of the astronomical archives of the Egyptians. This is the oldest recorded date that I know of. Next to it are the dates of the cave paintings in Lascaux and Altamira going back at least 27,000 years. The age of Tiahuanaco seems to be the same, but we have no precise data. But in 839 B.C. Babylonian priests recorded the start of the first Babylonian dynasty after the first deluge at the very early date of 24,989 B.C. Next in line of recorded documents is the indication in the Vatican Codex that the first Mayan calendar started in 18,633 B.C. The last cycle, begun in 3144 B.C., is to end in the year 2020 of our era.

The Aztecs counted their time in the same way as the Mayas, by the conjunctions of Jupiter and Saturn, but their cycles and the departure dates of these cycles were different. If the translations in the Vatican Codex are correct, we live now in the fifth cycle since the creation of the world. The first Aztec cycle, according to the same Vatican source, should have lasted 202 conjunctions of Jupiter and Saturn, or 4,011½ years and ended in a fantastic deluge that drowned everything and everybody. The second cycle of equal duration ended again in a catastrophe of violent cyclones that brought total destruction. The third period of the Aztec calendar lasted 242 conjunctions of the two planets, or 4,805 years and was finished by volcanic eruptions that burned everything to a crisp. The fourth cycle of 253 conjunctions or 5,024 years ended in general famine and starvation. We live now in the fifth Aztec time cycle which began in 781 B.C. and should end in our year 2020, significantly the same date as given by the Mayan calendar, though not telling us what to expect at that time. If we take the starting date of 781 B.C. and go back 17,852 years, the sum of the first four Aztec periods, we arrive at the same first year of the Mayan calendar—18,633 B.C.

Further, we have the date that is common in two different and widely separated cultures, the Mayan and the Hindu. It is the year 11,654 B.C. The Hindus counted time in periods of 2,850 years or 150 Metonic cycles of nineteen solar years each. According to my calculations their calendar started in 3104 B.C. If we go back three Hindu time-counting periods of 2,850 years each we arrive at the year 11,654 B.C. The Mayas counted time by several different methods, one of them being cycles of 2,760⅓ years that started in the year 3373 B.C. Three such cycles bring us back by exactly one year less than the date of the Hindu time-counting—the famous year 11,653 B.C.

Then there is the date of 11,540 B.C. that is common to the Egyptians and the Assyrians. The Egyptians counted by periods of 1,460 years and started one of their cycles in the year 5700 B.C. Four of these Egyptian cycles bring us back to 11,540 B.C. The Assyrians counted in periods of 95 Metonic cycles of nineteen solar years each, or cycles of 1,805 years starting in 710 B.C. Six of these periods result in the same date—the year 11,540 B.C., with the start year of the last cycle in 710 B.C.

The date for the creation of the world, according to Zoroaster the year 9657 B.C., is very close to the year 9564 B.C., the year when, according to the Tibetans, Atlantis sank.

After that we arrive at more recent dates like the Mayan date of 8307 B.C., opening year of the Mahabharata, the great epic of ancient India, in 7116 B.C. Then there are the calendars of the

Byzantines, Scandinavians, and Hebrews. Most of these ancient dates have been known for centuries but nobody dared to use or publish them because Irish Archbishop Ussher of Armagh, who propounded a biblical chronology in the seventeenth century, had established that the world was created in the year 4004 B.C. at nine o'clock in the morning of October 26, and for centuries it seemed imprudent to doubt such Bible wisdom.

Now the times have changed and the oldest known dates are used by quite a few people. Different authors publish them, and sometimes their dates differ slightly because they use varying methods of calculation. Nevertheless, when all the data are sorted out by computer, only three systems of counting time emerge: the lunar-solar method, the method using the sun and Sirius, and the reckoning by the conjunctions of Jupiter and Saturn.

We can see now that the universal calendar did exist many thousands of years ago. We have only rediscovered it. It was based on the conjunctions of Jupiter and Saturn, and the Mayas could start their calendar with the year 18,633 B.C. by continuing the same system that started the Egyptian time-counting or the time-counting of the Egyptian predecessors 49,214 years before our era—always in whole number of the two-planet conjunctions.

Out of sheer curiosity, I wanted to calculate intermediary dates by intervals of ten Jupiter-Saturn conjunctions of 198.6 years each. Since I am convinced that we will continue to discover older documented dates as we progress in our research and probably reach and surpass the date of the Nineveh Constant 64,800 years ago, I made up a calendar of thirteen great Mayan cycles counting back from the end of the present one which will end in the year 2020. The thirteen cycles of 5,163 years each brought me to 65,100 years B.C.

CHAPTER 10

The Four Moons

THERE IS ONE ABSOLUTELY fantastic astronomical theory proposed quite a while ago by Hoerbiger and confirmed recently by Hans Bellamy and Peter Allen, stating that during its lifetime of several billion years, our earth captured four moons one after another. Three of them exploded as they crashed on earth creating the three biggest oceans—the Atlantic, the Pacific, and the Indian—and destroying all living things. The fourth moon is our present one that still hangs in the skies.

This theory, seen as science fiction by most scientists, would not have been discussed in this book if I had not myself discovered some surprising new facts that seem to confirm it. When I first heard of Hoerbiger's theory, I did think the poor man had lost his marbles. But then I remembered that once everybody regarded the German physicist Alfred Wegener's theory of the floating continents as pure fiction until much later discoveries proved his concept was true, precise, and prophetic.

So I reconsidered the possibility that our planet might have had more than one moon in the past and that Bellamy and Allen might be proven right even if we simply keep in mind that nothing in our universe is stable and that everything is in constant change and movement.

It is evident that our present moon has not always been at the same distance from earth as it is today. Unfortunately, our science dictates that this distance must have been greater in the past than now, because all satellites descend in a very slow spiral toward the planet around which they rotate. This is caused by the deceleration due to friction with cosmic dust. The smaller satellites lose their distance faster than the bigger ones, which have more favorable ratios of mass to the area of their cross sections. But there is a contradiction here. While the laws of celestial mechanics tell us that the moon in the past must have been farther from earth than today, legends and sacred texts from all corners of the globe tell us the opposite—that the moon in the past was bigger and closer to us. It even looked much bigger than the sun. How do we solve this puzzle? Well, let's start by examining the known facts.

In the ranges of the Andes at an altitude of 12,000 feet geologists have found stretches of marine sediment reaching 640 km all the way from Peru to Bolivia, clear evidence beyond any doubt that the level of the ocean only some tens of thousands of years ago was 12,000 feet higher there than today. Similar sediments, dating from the same geological period, have also been found in the Himalayas, in South Asia.

A geologist would be tempted to say right away that it wasn't the sea but the mountains of Peru and Bolivia that rose to this level, because the tectonic plate supporting the Cordillera range was pushed upward. But the sediment line is relatively recent compared to the millions of years since the Andes were created. So it must be the sea that once rose, as it still does all around the world twice every day, except that once there was a gigantic pull that made the sea climb 12,000 feet in a huge bulging ring around the equator. And such force could only have been produced by a big celestial body very close to the earth. It must have been a closer and larger moon whose gravitational force pulled most of the water from all oceans into that bulging ring, like a gigantic, permanent tidal wave.

Some people think it was the planet Venus that passed very close to earth in the past. And it certainly does seem true that Venus has not always been part of our solar system. Some think the phenomenon was caused by a moon, not necessarily the first one our planet had. Both theories may be right and it is even possible that both Venus and our moon combined forces to raise the highest tides the world ever experienced. But let's discuss the moon first.

As I said before, the theory of a very close and very big moon explains the marine sediments at the 12,000-foot elevation most logically. Such a supermoon would have enough pull to nearly balance the gravity of the earth. Together with the spin of the earth, it would cause immense tides in the Torrid Zone, and if this moon would create four tides during one day, as would be the case with a moon spinning fast enough, there would be no time for the tides to ebb away. The high-water belt on the equator would become a stationary and permanent feature with the resulting accumulation of marine sediment at this high level.

But since it is impossible that our present moon could have been at any time closer to earth than it is now and since it is also improbable that it would have been much bigger in the not so distant past, we must assume that there must have been another moon, bigger and closer to earth, before we started serenading our present little one. And if there could have been two moons, why not three or four? The theory of the four moons is not so crazy after all. It seems to be quite sane, because it is in harmony with all the legends and especially with the mysterious stories about giants who lived at the time of the big moon. Even the Bible tells us about them.

We have another mystery to solve. What's the relation between the existence of giants on earth in the past that nobody, including even the Church, has ever doubted, and the closer and bigger moon? In my opinion, there is a clear cause-and-effect relationship. While our official science still dismisses the multiple-moon theory, it is not quite so sure there isn't a direct influence of gravity, among other factors, upon the size of the human body. The Watusi of East Africa are much taller than the Eskimos, and it could be that this difference is caused by dissimilar gravity, which is less at the equator than at the poles. But the aborigines of Australia who live close to the equator are very small and so are the people in Borneo and Sumatra, who live right on it. There must be other causes that determine our size, like radioactivity or availability of food. Disregarding these contradictions, we must however recognize that there is a direct cause-and-effect relationship between gravity and human size, that seems indeed to be limited by the weight of the body that our limbs can carry.

A powerful, close, and big moon would have reduced the weight of the human body more in the Torrid Zone and on the equator than in Temperate or Frigid zones. It so happens that in Tiahuanaco, which is in the Torrid Zone, giant human skulls have been discovered that must have belonged to humans nine to ten feet tall. In China, Java, Morocco, Tunisia, and Syria archaeologists have found flint hand tools and flint weapons weighing 10 to 22 pounds. Only giants could have made and used such tools and weapons.

Nobody denies the existence of giant animals in the past. We have the bones to prove it. And even if at the present we have only a few skulls and tibias of giant men and not too many of their tools, there is little reason to dismiss the theory of nearby moons and giants on the earth. It is only natural that first there were giant animals and then huge men. The theory of evolution of the species still has its validity, but with a correcting factor of gravitation.

Until quite recently, the theory of the four moons was supported only by the findings of Bellamy and Allen, whose book *The Calendar of Tiahuanaco* caused much discussion in the scientific world. Some doubted the conclusions the authors arrived at because the crux of the matter—the hieroglyphics on the Gate of the Sun—were only partially deciphered. That is true, but in my opinion the interpretation of Allen and Bellamy, apart from some unimportant errors, was quite exact and their data from the Gate of the Sun have been confirmed by numbers that I have found from other sources.

The ancient builders of Tiahuanaco, in Bolivia, who are unknown to us, apparently feared that the Gate of the Sun, which carries the hieroglyphics constituting their calendar, might be destroyed in a catastrophe. It was not destroyed although the disaster did come about. By the greatest of miracles, the stone gate was found face down in a dried-out bed of clay about 300 ft from its foundations. The clay cover saved the mysterious markings on the stone face from erosion and so to this day the hieroglyphics are in an excellent state of preservation.

However, to be prepared in case the Gate of the Sun, with its engraved calendar might be destroyed, the architects and astronomers of Tiahuanaco built a huge monument that also incorporated their calendar and all the astronomical descriptions of the relative positions of planets and their satellites known at that time. This superb and unique monument is the Temple of Kalasasaya, inside which the fallen Gate of the Sun was found. Nobody, so it seems, ever realized that the dimensions and the layout of Kalasasaya Temple duplicated the Tiahuanaco calendar. But according to my calculations, which differ only slightly from those made by Bellamy and Allen, the relationships between the sun, our planet earth, and the moon at the time Tiahuanaco was built were the following: The moon circled the earth 36 times faster than now. According to the laws of Kepler, the distance from the earth of the fast circling moon was only 5½ terrestrial radii, or about 35,250 km, 10.903 times closer than our moon is now.

This proximity of the moon and the enormous tides it produced slowed the rotation of the earth down to 288 turns per year, compared to our present 365 turns, so that the year then had only 288 days. However, the time our earth needed to rotate around the sun was not affected and remained at 8,766 hours of 3,600 seconds each. All other time periods were, naturally, quite different.

Since we are now living in the era of the electronic pocket calculator and many may find amusement in checking numbers, I will give here the precise astronomical periods that were the cornerstones of the Tiahuanaco calendar. These periods are indicated by three dimensions of the Kalasasaya Temple. Its length of 288 cubits corresponds to the number of days in a solar year. The width of 264 cubits corresponds to the number of days in a lunar year. The distance of 156 cubits from the western extremity of the terrace to the observation point, which will be discussed later in this chapter, gives us the number of eclipses in a solar year and, consequently, indicates the number of synodic revolutions of the moon, which was 444 at that time.

If we divide 8,766, the number of hours in one solar year, by these numbers we obtain a solar year of 288 days, each day having 30.4375 hours and 444 lunar synodic periods of 19.7432 hours each. The lunar year that we obtain from these values is 264

TIAHUANACO RUINS

General Map in Cubits of 445.851 mm

PRESENT NORTH

TEMPLETE
104x112

AKAPANA
288x396

KALASASAYA
264x288

LAKAKOLU
88x96

PUTUNI
96x120

KERIKALA
78x120

| 0 | 100 | 200 | 300 | 400 | CUBITS |

| 0 | 50 | 100 | 150 | 200 | METERS |

PANTHEON
48x56

days, or 8,035.5 hours, corresponding to 407 synodic periods of
the moon while it goes through all its phases. The number of
eclipses in one year is 156 cycles for the solar year and 143 cycles
for the lunar year.

Exactly as the width of the temple represents 11/12 of its
length, so the lunar year represents 11/12 of a solar year. This
fact alone seems to confirm the interpretation of the Gate of the
Sun numbers and the Tiahuanaco calendar, and the theory of the
four moons does not seem so improbable any more. In fact, it begins to look very probable.

The Tiahuanaco astronomers worked with a small time cycle
of 3,168 days, representing 11 solar years or 12 lunar years. Apparently, they also worked with a great cycle of 9,504 days,
which was the time the sun and the moon needed to come to the
same longitude and the same point on the zodiac of that period
in our planet's history.

Some might ask how the Nineveh Constant fits in with the
theory of the four moons, when the intervals were of different
value. So check again with your handy calculator—it fits with
precision up to the fifth decimal point. Start with the number of
hours in the Nineveh Constant, which is 54,432 million, or exactly
6,209,445 solar years of 8,766 hours each, or 1,788,320,160 days of
30.4375 hours of that time. Equally precise are the numbers that
you will obtain from the division of the Nineveh Constant into
564,495 cycles of 11 solar years or 12 lunar years.

Now the Temple of Kalasasaya in Tiahuanaco is built at an altitude of 3,845 m and situated at 16°27' south latitude and 68°41'
west longitude. One degree of longitude at this latitude is about
106,790 m. Dividing this by 360,000, we obtain a local foot of
0.296639 m, very close to the actual foot of 0.297234 m, which
will play an important role in this story.

Kalasasaya is in ruins now. But it was built on a stone masonry
terrace that has kept its form and dimensions fairly well. It is

This map shows the orientations and the dimensions of the principal
ruins measured in Tiahuanaco cubits of 445.851 millimeters each. The
width-to-length ratios of several buildings had astronomical or mathematical meanings. For example, 264 and 288 were the numbers of
days in the lunar and solar years at that time, and 288/396 was the
tangent of 36 degrees.

KALASASAYA TEMPLE IN TIAHUANACO

Original Dimensions in Meters

117.70 meters

NORTH

Main Gate

128.40 meters

Observation
Point

288 cubits

156 cubits or 69 ½ meters

Puerta del Sol

El Fraile

Western Gallery

77 cubits

110 cubits

77 cubits

34.33 meters

49.04 meters

34.33 meters

117.70 meters
264 cubits

This map shows the original dimensions of the Temple of Kalasasaya
in meters and in Tiahuanaco cubits of 445.851 millimeters each. The
famous Gate of the Sun and the idol called El Fraile are shown in
their present locations; nobody knows exactly where they were before
the destruction of the temple.

oriented lengthwise approximately from west to east as were most ancient monuments, to be in line with the sun, and measures 128.40 by 117.70 m. On its western end the temple has a gallery of eleven stone pillars made of the hardest locally available stone, andesite. This gallery is placed 4.16 m outside the western end of the terrace and the pillars erected at unequal intervals are of varying width. The distance between the axes of the first and last pillars is 32.70 m and the outward borders of these two are at 33.30 m from each other. The height of these stone slabs was about 4 m. Nine of them are erect, leaning about 2 degrees westward, the fifth pillar, counting from south, has been displaced by about 200 m westward while the tenth has been toppled over next to its foundation. The sizes and intervals of these tall stones we will analyze later, determining their astronomical values.

The north face of the terrace is in poor shape, but can be reconstructed easily because it is identical to the south side, which is better preserved. This side has twenty-nine pillars of limestone, which are more eroded than the andesite pillars on the west. The length of the stonework terrace on which the temple was built is divided by these twenty-nine pillars into twenty-eight equal parts of 4.60 m each. The east end of the terrace was divided into 28 equal parts of 4.20 m each. It is possible that originally, before the western outside gallery was built, that that face of the temple was divided into twenty-four equal intervals of 4.90 m, divided by twenty-five pillars.

All these numbers and divisions sound complicated, but we will see that every dimension had its reason for being and every one was a multiple, sometimes with a slight fraction, of the local foot of 0.297234 m and the cubit of 0.445851 m, or 1½ local feet. The cubit was divided into seven hands of 0.063693 m and each hand divided into four fingers measuring 0.015923 m each. As can be seen on the god figure carved in the Puerta del Sol, the gods of Tiahuanaco had only four digits each on their hands and their feet.

Thus the cubit was equal to twenty-eight fingers, just like the twenty-eight intervals between the pillars of the north, east, and south façades of the temple. The only difference shown by the length of the intervals themselves was that the east intervals were of 264 fingers each—the count of days in the lunar year, while the north and south intervals of 288 fingers each—the number of days in the solar year.

The same numbers are contained in the hieroglyphics in the Tiahuanaco calendar and they are nearly the same as the figures Bellamy and Allen arrived at in their calculations: 264 and 290 instead of 288, an error caused by the proportion that they used, namely 10:11 instead of the 11:12 I chose because 264 and 288 divided by 24 makes 11 and 12. This proportion, by the way, expressed as a trigonometric function of cosine, is very close to that of 23.450 degrees, the inclination angle of our planet, which could have been 23.556 degrees at that time.

The Tiahuanaco foot, as calculated by the dimensions of the temple, does not correspond exactly to the local foot as I calculated it from the geographical co-ordinates. But the difference is only 0.000595 m, or slightly less than $\frac{6}{10}$ of 1 mm, which could be caused by no less than four different reasons. First, it could be that our ancestors did a poor calculation, which seems to be out of the question, judging by all the other calculations they made routinely and exactly. The second reason might be the altitude or the irregularity of the local formation of the earth's crust, which seems to bulge, giving a longer degree at Tiahuanaco than at sea level. This deformation must have been even greater when the big moon caused the belt around the equator. The third possibility is that Tiahuanaco was part of a large empire, and the local degree was taken from a center 42 km further north, from a latitude 16.07° south. It would be really curious to find prehistoric ruins at the latter latitude some day. The fourth and most believable explanation is that since Tiahuanaco was built and its calendar calculated, the equator has moved north by 23 minutes of arc.

No matter what the explanation, the foot of Tiahuanaco of 0.297234 m is the correct value. Bellamy and Allen themselves estimated the Tiahuanaco cubit at 0.4458 m, which gives a foot of 0.2972 m. Another proof that these values are true is the weight that can be derived from the Tiahuanaco foot—26,260 gm, which is exactly the weight of 1 talent of gold or silver used for thousands of years throughout the Mediterranean basin.

Does that prove that trade existed between these ancient cultures, or is it just proof that both cultures had common roots?

Now that we know the exact dimensions of the cubit, the foot, and the finger, it is interesting to go back to the andesite pillars of the western gallery and try to find out what the dimensions there tell us. It does not make any sense to give dimensions in our metric system, because our modern units of measurement do not give the numbers 7, 9, 11, 12, and 13, numbers that fit exactly in the layout of the temple to reflect the astronomical values we are interested in. Here are nine dimensions, all in cubits, that can simultaneously help to explain the irregularity of the spaces between pillars and prove that at the time these pillars were set there was in the sky a moon much larger and much closer than our present one. Since of the eleven pillars, the outer two are there only to frame the field of vision, let's look at the nine possible combinations of the nine spaces between the inner pillars and each time add the pillar's own width to the distance. Thus we obtain the following measurements in cubits: 20¼, 19, 19, 18, 18¼, 17¼, 19¼, 17¾, 19¼.

We now have seven different intervals, two of them repeated twice, probably to measure something very big, like a moon so close to earth that it would vary in its apparent diameter because of the elliptic path it was describing in the sky. But it does not take long to discover that if an observer places himself 170 cubits from the pillars, the angles from there represented by the above intervals read, starting from the south, 7°, 6°40′, 6°40′, 6°20′, 6°30′, 6°, 6°50′, 6°10′, 6°50′, giving a total for the observation field of 59°. The average apparent diameter of the moon at that time must have been 6½°, or 11.68 per cent bigger than the diameter that we calculated from the laws of celestial mechanics for our present moon, namely, 5.82°. We can conclude that the moon of that period was 12 per cent larger than the present one.

We have yet to talk about an additional problem tied in with the theory of the four moons, the age of Tiahuanaco. One way to estimate its age would be to use the climatic cycle of 21,000 years that we discussed when we talked about ice ages in Chapter 1. This cycle is the time period needed for the date of the equinox to arrive at the same moment when the sun is at its perigee—the point closest to earth. If we want to believe the

KALASASAYA TEMPLE IN TIAHUANACO

THE NINE POSITIONS OF THE MOON 27,000 YEARS AGO

OBSERVED BETWEEN THE PILLARS OF THE WESTERN GALLERY

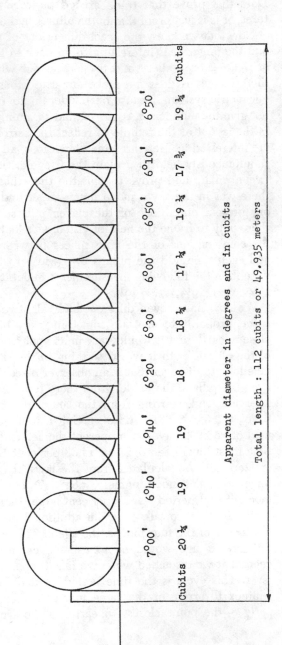

7°00'	6°40'	6°40'	6°20'	6°30'	6°00'	6°50'	6°10'	6°50'
Cubits 20 ⅝	19	19	18	18 ½	17 ½	19 ¼	17 ¾	19 ½ Cubits

Apparent diameter in degrees and in cubits

Total length : 112 cubits or 49.935 meters

code breakers of the Tiahuanaco calendar, this timetable was calculated on the date when the spring equinox in the southern hemisphere coincided with the sun in perigee, a situation that last occurred 6,000 years ago and, before that, 27,000 years earlier.

Now, the Tiahuanaco calendar could not possibly have been calculated only 6,000 years ago. The ruins are obviously much older than that, and also, all the legends from 4000 B.C. tell us that our present moon was already there, shining bright and silvery.

So we must believe that the true age of the Tiahuanaco calendar is about 27,000 years, about the same as the cave paintings of Lascaux and Altamira.

What is even more surprising is the fact that the numbers 264 and 288 were used by other ancient civilizations in South America, and that the phenomenon of the big moon was known throughout Central America.

In the region of Cuenca, in Equador, Juan Moricz found buried caves in 1965 that until then had been known only to the local Indians. His information is very scant and inaccessible, but the discoverer reported that the central hall of treasures of these caves has dimensions of 137.7 by 150.2 m, proportional to 264 and 288, numbers that I found and that will not be known to anybody till this book is published. Another surprise is that these two dimensions of the hall of treasures in the Cuenca caves correspond exactly to the local foot of 0.3476 m and the cubit derived from it of 0.5214 m. These dimensions are real and we will find them later. They also give us the precise length of 1 degree of longitude at 2½° south latitude, which is nearly the latitude of Cuenca.

Father Crespi runs the local gold museum in Cuenca. He has been a lifelong friend of the local Indians and custodian of the treasures that are brought to him by his Indian friends when they need something. Most of the objects in the Cuenca museum are pure gold and of extraordinary beauty. The masterpiece is a

This illustration shows the eleven pillars of the western gallery and the nine positions of the moon that could be observed between them about 27,000 years ago, when the moon was much closer to the earth.

golden plate 52 cm long, 14 wide, and 4 thick. Next to it is a weeping god, also solid gold, 52 cm high, which happens to be the length of the local cubit. And the god's hands and feet have only four fingers, like the god of Tiahuanaco.

Strange coincidences? A cubit of longitide, the hall in the caves, the gold tablet, and the gold idol with four fingers: that makes four times the same measurement appears, which we will call the Cuenca cubit of 0.5214 m. When we divide it by 28 we obtain one finger of 18.62 mm.

The gold plate of the Cuenca museum keeps surprising me. At first it seemed to be only a standard of length. Then it looked also like a unit of volume of $28 \times 2 \times 7.5$ fingers, or 420 cubic fingers. Finally, with a specific gravity of 19.37 for the very pure Inca gold, it certainly was a unit of weight of 52,520 grams, or 2 gold talents from the Mediterranean. Now, call *that* a coincidence!

So far none of the fifty-six hieroglyphs has been deciphered. It could be an alphabet of fifty-six letters. It could be a lunar calendar of fifty-six years. It could be anything else. We simply do not know. But these discoveries have already told us that the civilizations of Tiahuanaco and Cuenca had more than just the four-fingered gods in common. And we also find the same basic numbers in Monte Albán and Teotihuacán, in Mexico.

The sunken court in Monte Albán measures 78.50 by 85.60 m, or exactly 264 by 288 Tiahuanaco ft, even though the two sites are separated by thousands of kilometers. Even more surprising are the pyramids of Teotihuacán whose dimensions again are based on the two sacred numbers. The Pyramid of the Moon seems to be 128.3 by 152.6 m, which could represent 264 by 288 Teotihuacán yd of 1.060 m each. Nobody seems to know the exact dimensions of the base of the Pyramid of the Sun, which is still covered with rubble. However, the measurements at Teotihuacán are a very controversial issue. I have three recent books on the subject and they all give different numbers. Only one thing seems almost certain. If we divide 2,400 m, the length of the Grand Avenue, by the Teotihuacán yard of 1.0582 m, we obtain the Nineveh Constant of 2,268. Is that another coincidence?

In short, we have convincing evidence that four separate American civilizations used the same numbers and the same units of measurement to express the two sacred numbers of astronomy that had the greatest importance for them, the numbers of days in the lunar and in the solar year at that time.

There is another even more mysterious example of the use of the same sacred numbers on the other side of the world, namely, at the famed Tower of Babel. It was constructed, in units of the

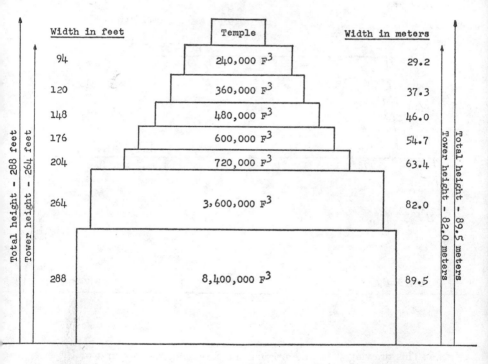

THE TOWER OF BABEL

Original Dimensions in Meters
and in Sumerian Feet of 310.723 mm

Width in feet	Temple	Width in meters
94	240,000 F^3	29.2
120	360,000 F^3	37.3
148	480,000 F^3	46.0
176	600,000 F^3	54.7
204	720,000 F^3	63.4
264	3,600,000 F^3	82.0
288	8,400,000 F^3	89.5

(left margin) Total height - 288 feet   Tower height - 264 feet

(right margin) Total height - 89.5 meters   Tower height - 82.0 meters

This drawing shows the original dimensions of the Tower of Babel in meters and in Sumerian feet of 0.310723 meters. The tower was built with 57.6 million bricks and its volume of 14,400,000 cubic feet, or 432,000 cubic meters, was ⅙ of the volume of the Great Pyramid of Cheops. In Babylon, 432,000 was also the length in years of the Great Year, and the ratio of 264:288 was the same as the one used at Kalasasaya in Tiahuanaco.

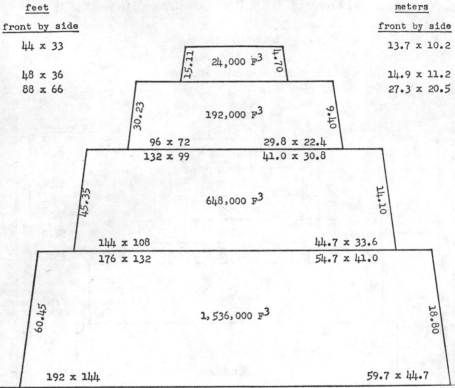

THE ZIGGURAT OF UR

Original Dimensions in Meters

and in Sumerian Feet of 310.723 mm

feet		meters
front by side		front by side
44 x 33		13.7 x 10.2
48 x 36		14.9 x 11.2
88 x 66		27.3 x 20.5

15.11   24,000 F³   4.70

30.23   192,000 F³   9.40

96 x 72   29.8 x 22.4
132 x 99   41.0 x 30.8

45.35   648,000 F³   14.10

144 x 108   44.7 x 33.6
176 x 132   54.7 x 41.0

60.45   1,536,000 F³   18.80

192 x 144   59.7 x 44.7

This drawing shows the original dimensions of the Ziggurat of Ur, in meters and in Sumerian feet of 0.310723 meters. It was built with 9.6 million bricks and its volume was 2.4 million cubic feet, or 720,-000 cubic meters, which represented ⅙ of the volume of the Tower of Babel, or ⅟₃₆ of that of the Great Pyramid of Cheops. The first tier has a 132:144 ratio equal to 264:288.

Sumerian foot of 0.319723 m, out of 57.6 million clay bricks, each with a volume of 0.25 cu ft. The volume of the whole tower was 14.4 million cu ft, or 432,000 cu m, six times smaller than the Cheops pyramid. The tower was 264 ft tall, and on its top stood the 24-ft-high Temple of Marduk, making the total height of the tower 288 ft. The statue of Marduk was cast in solid gold and weighed 800 Sumerian talents, or 24 metric tons.

It really seems that the Tower of Babel was built with the Tiahuanaco proportion of 264:288 because not only its measurements in height but also the proportion of the two first terraces is such. Its total volume of 432,000 cu m ties it in with the metric system and with the number of 432,000 years, which is used even today by the descendants of the ancient Hindus as an astronomical and religious time cycle. The Babylonians used the same cycle, but divided it by 40, creating the time cycle of 10,800 years, which is found in many cultures. As for the Ziggurat of Ur, its volume is ⅙ of the Tower of Babel, or $\frac{1}{36}$ of the Great Pyramid of Cheops. Also, the surface of its first terrace was 2,268 sq m!

We must recognize here, whether we like it or not, that widely separated cultures used similar systems for measuring length, volume, weight, and time, standards whose original sources have disappeared without recognizable trace. Yet the common heritage seems incontestable, and if we want to believe the Egyptian, Tibetan, and many other legends, the common source of all culture was a great island in the middle of the Atlantic ocean that disappeared in the waves 12,000 years ago, the fabled Atlantis, which we will discuss next.

CHAPTER 11

The Mystery of Atlantis

AROUND 580 B.C., WHEN the Athenian statesman Solon had finished compiling the code of law that made him immortal, he took a long vacation and went to Saïs, then the capital of Lower Egypt. Saïs was the center of culture at that time and people of fame and talent used to congregate there to hone their intellects. It was there that Solon met the high priest of Egypt, Sonchis, who very generously showed him the greatest part of the famed Egyptian archives, dating back many thousands of years, and also told him a fascinating story about a terrible disaster that had occurred 9,000 years before. It was the story of the sunken continent of Atlantis.

This legend, which is still considered by many as pure mythology, was retold by Solon to his nephew Dropides, who in turn transmitted it to his descendants, one of whom told it to the philosopher Plato. Two of Plato's most famous works, *Timaeus* and *Critias*, have preserved most of the legend of Atlantis in all its passionate and tragic greatness.

Personally I am convinced that the story of Atlantis, as Solon heard it from Sonchis and as Plato has given it to us, is true from beginning to end and that some day the ruins of Atlantis will be found, just as one after another we found the once legendary Troy, Mycenae, Tiryns, and Knossos. Meanwhile, we can look at the information that has been assembled about Atlantis and the catastrophe that made it disappear.

According to Sonchis, 9,000 years before his time there was an immense island in the middle of the Atlantic Ocean, due west of the Pillars of Hercules, now called the Strait of Gibraltar. This island was bigger than all of North Africa and the Near East put together. Its name was Atlantis and it was inhabited by very advanced people of unknown origin, who were great mathematicians, astronomers, land cultivators, and masters in metallurgy. Their capital city, Poseidonis, was named after the god of the sea, Poseidon, and built in the middle of a vast plain, protected by mountain chains and connected with the ocean by a man-made waterway 600 ft wide and 100 ft deep. The canal ringed the entire city and served not only for local transportation but also for ocean-going vessels. The fields around Poseidonis were rich with crops, and horses, cattle, and elephants grazed there. Atlantis was protected both from east and west by a maze of small islands, and navigators had to go through these archipelagoes to come to the fabled place.

Atlantis had lived many thousands of years in peace and prosperity until one day the leadership of the land was taken over by a military clique that decided to conquer all the people who lived around the Mediterranean. The generals of Atlantis raised an army of 750,000 men and many war chariots and easily conquered both sides of the Mediterranean, all of southern Europe except Greece, and all of North Africa except Egypt. Then they decided to push forward and make their victory total by smashing Greece and Egypt.

At that time the highly cultured Egyptians were no match for the invader, but the best warriors of that era, the Greeks, saved the Egyptians by winning decisive victories over the invaders. They even liberated all the conquered Mediterranean lands. When the invader fled, the Greeks put together an expeditionary army and sent it to Poseidonis to make sure that there would be no new invasions. It was while the Greeks were in Poseidonis that, within one day and one night, powerful earthquakes and devastating tides destroyed Atlantis. The prospering continent sank beneath the Atlantic Ocean. Both armies and all the people perished. And, according to the description that Sonchis gave

Solon, all that was left where once plains and mountains stretched to the horizon, was a huge morass and swamp, something like today's Sargasso Sea.

This detailed and dramatic story is probably one of the greatest recollections of mankind, but until recently it was very hard to take it for anything but legend. Today, however, we know many things not known until relatively recently. We know that human beings have been around for much more than 100,-000 years and highly civilized people existed for at least 12,000 years. We know that our continents float, that the poles shift, that levels of the oceans change, and that islands emerge and sink. It is no longer possible to say the legend of Atlantis is plain myth because the events it describes were impossible. To the contrary, the disappearance of Atlantis is now known to have been quite possible, geologically as well as historically.

But there is still serious argument as to where Atlantis was located before it disappeared, and for a while it was even believed that Atlantis was not Atlantis but the Aegean island of Thera (once called Santorin) and that the great earthquake that made Atlantis disappear in the sea was actually the eruption in 1521 B.C. of the volcano on Thera.

The Thera argument won't stand up for several reasons. First, if Atlantis really disappeared in 1521 B.C., how come the Bible doesn't say anything about it? This was 700 years after the death of Abraham and about 100 years before the birth of Moses, when the Hebrews undoubtedly had mastered the art of keeping written records.

Next, if the disappearance of Atlantis had taken place in the Aegean Sea only 940 years before Solon lived, everybody in Greece would have known it, especially Solon, who was a very learned man. He would have known it just as most educated people today know that England was invaded by the Normans in 1066, even though it happened 910 years ago.

Equally improbable is the possibility that Atlantis, being larger than all of North Africa and the Near East together, could have been anywhere in the Mediterranean. And certainly a small island like Thera could never have mobilized 750,000 men. Nor have any remains of elephants been found in Thera. And finally we know that Atlantis disappeared after a series of earthquakes, not in a volcanic eruption, which is a completely different kind of event.

Another much more likely theory postulates that the continents of North and South America together was the fabled Atlantis. Now, this total area is indeed as big as all of North Africa and the Near East together and indeed there were elephants roaming the plains in America 12,000 years ago. Also, both Americas are rich in metal ores as Atlantis was, and there are many islands along both coasts.

Finally, this new theory is partially based on recent discoveries that Hindus and Phoenicians had agricultural colonies in eastern Mexico where cotton and jute were cultivated 2,900 years ago, and even older are the Sumerian and Phoenician copper and tin mines in Peru and Bolivia, which may also have produced gold and silver as long as 4,300 years ago. Inscriptions resembling the Cretan linear writing have been found in cliffs of the Upper Amazon, indicating that sailors from the Aegean passed that way on regular trade routes.

However, even these finds don't seem quite old enough to fit the mystery of Atlantis. They go back to only about 1,700 years before Solon, which is not the time of the disappearance of the fabled island. Therefore it seems much more likely that, instead of covering both Americas, Atlantis was only located in the central part of the area, from Florida to the estuary of Amazon, which would be southwest of Gibraltar, or the Pillars of Hercules.

The Tibetan bible, the Book of Dzyan, which goes back to the very farthest past, records that in the year 9564 B.C. a very large part of the earth sank into the ocean in what is now the Caribbean and the Gulf of Mexico. History does not tell us how the Tibetans of that time, on the other side of the world, learned about this cataclysmic event, but it is possible that they got it from the best source—refugees from Atlantis, who went all the way to Tibet to make sure they were on firm ground that wouldn't disappear beneath the waves again. Main thing is, that the date of the catastrophe was precisely and exactly recorded and preserved, and the Tibetan record of Atlantis dovetails nicely with Solon's account, so we have no reason to doubt it. And as for the location of Atlantis, if one studies a map of the waters surrounding the American continents, none could be more probable. It is easy to trace the east coast of the sunken Atlantis along the line drawn from Florida to the Bahamas, Hispaniola, Puerto Rico, the Antilles, Trinidad, and the north coast of South America from the estuary of the Orinoco to that of the Amazon. And now new discoveries made at the center of this region offer indisputable proofs and final evidence that Atlantis really existed.

It is possible that the actual rediscovery of Atlantis began in 1967, when Robert Brush, an American pilot and archaeologist, flying at low altitude near Bimini in the Bahamas noticed a huge rectangular form a few feet below the water. He photographed it right away.

Now, the first law of the fundamental code of underwater archaeology states that water and waves can create all kinds of strange forms from the sand or rocks on the bottom but never a rectangle with four right angles. The second law states that any such form invariably belongs to an ancient temple, usually surrounded by smaller rectangles or circles, which were the habitats of the priests, servants, or pilgrims.

Brush called in Dimitri Rebikoff, a professional diver and archaeologist, who had spent twenty years in underwater archaeology in the Mediterranean and was considered the most experienced and qualified scientist in this category. He recognized the importance of the discovery right away. He himself had photographed from a plane an immense submerged rectangle 400 m long off the Grand Bank of Bermuda, as well as other remnants of human construction along a straight line or grouped in circles in an area covering over 30 miles between Orange Cay and Bimini in the Bahamas. Rebikoff in turn asked Professor Manson Valentine, who had discovered important Mayan ruins in Yucatán, to join in an expedition to Bimini and the surrounding islands.

In August of 1968 this expedition discovered a 75-by-90-foot temple of very great age off the coast of Andros, the largest island in the Bahamas. But the most important discovery came on September 2, 1968, when at the northwest extremity of North Bimini, under only 15 feet of water, Valentine found a vast expanse of pavement made of flat, rectangular and polygonal stone slabs. All were hand-cut and without doubt man-made. The stone slabs had been submerged for many thousands of years, as evidenced by their corners, which had been rounded by the movement of sand over a very, very long time. The biggest slabs were 9 to 15 ft long and formed the whole width of the paved avenues, and in some spots more than one layer of stones had been used.

The size and form of these slabs, as well as the precise cuts and joints, reminded one of the stone slab ruins on both sides of the Atlantic—the Giza and Baalbek monuments, in Egypt and Lebanon, respectively, and the temples of Cuzco and Tiahuanaco, in Bolivia. Along the coast of Andros at a depth of 150 ft the French undersea explorer Jacques Cousteau has found a huge stalactite and stalagmite cave, a type of cave that could only have been formed by drops of lime water falling over long periods of time in free air, not under water. And the sediment in this cave is about 12,000 years old.

During the same expedition Cousteau explored the Blue Hole, a deep abyss near the coast of Belize, in Central America, where he discovered a labyrinth of stalactite and stalagmite caves, all at an angle, which is contrary to the way these formations can grow. The only explanation is that a strong earthquake tilted these caves and their formations of calcite deposits. And again the analysis of the stalactites showed their age to be about 12,000 years.

This is clear evidence that some 12,000 years ago a large part of the American continent, now under the Caribbean Sea and the Gulf of Mexico, was inundated during a seismic catastrophe so that only the highest mountain peaks remained above water. These are, of course, the Caribbean islands of today.

All this sounds strangely similar to what the Book of Dzyan tells us about Atlantis. Everything is there, including the right date, 9564 B.C. And the location, too, is the same—the Gulf of Mexico, the Bahamian area of the Atlantic, and the Caribbean Sea. Is it still possible to assume that the authors of the Tibetan bible invented it? Personally I do not think so. I sincerely believe the ruins of human habitations on the submerged plateau off the Bahamas are indeed offering us the first indisputable evidence that Atlantis really existed and that at least part of this sunken continent was in that very area.

Also, if Atlantis had never existed, we would have to invent it to explain the many mysteries that are totally unexplainable otherwise. First, there is the mythological mystery. How is it that the gods of nearly all civilizations around the world came from the sea, like the Mayan god Kukulcan, after he had descended from the skies? His sarcophagus, which seems to have been discovered in Palenque, in southern Mexico, has the shape of a fish. The god Oannes emerged every day from the deep sea to teach the Sumerians assembled on the shore in order to listen and learn. We could also ask how come the gods arriving on the American continent always came from the east, while the gods coming to Europe always arrived from the west, all indications of one central Atlantic origin long since forgotten.

Then we have the mystery of the Atlantic dialects comparable to the dialects of the Mediterranean: a group of rough, guttural dialects still spoken, from the Guanche dialect of the Azores and the Canary Islands to the many tongues of unknown origin spoken between Morocco and Ireland. And the impossible-sounding names, even more difficult to write in our Greek-Latin alphabet, consisting of letters that we use very little, like x and z, found in places inhabited by the Bretons, the Basques, the Gaels, the Andalusians, and the Berbers. All of these mysterious languages are related to the Guanche dialect and dialects all the way across the Azores and the Canary Islands to the Mayan lands of the Yucatán with its areas of ancient religious centers like Chichén Itzá, Izamal, Tzebtun, Uxmal, Uxul, Yaxuna or Oxkintok.

There is the story of the Basque missionary, who arrived to plow the Fields of the Lord in Yucatán and discovered that the best way to make himself clear to the local Indians was to talk to them in his native tongue! Some day, when we decipher the mysterious ancient inscriptions found in the Azores and the Canary Islands, we might learn more about these languages, too. Even the Basques themselves are an unsolved enigma. Tall and strong, they have all the characteristics of the Cro-Magnon people who emerged suddenly about 65,000 years ago, while the lesser Neanderthal man continued to exist for a while longer. Could the Cro-

Magnons have been colonists from Atlantis, who established their new homes in Europe and survived there the destruction of their land of origin, continuing the culture that they had brought along?

Besides, the Basques have a blood type and Rh factor combination that is extremely rare and can be found only along the shores of the Atlantic Ocean in people speaking the unknown dialects. The same blood types are found in Egyptian and Inca mummies. That could explain why the Incas and the pharaohs cultivated marriages between brothers and sisters—in order to preserve the rare blood that was not of this world, so it seems, because no other humans have it in such pure form.

In 1952 two British scientists analyzed the blood of five Inca mummies discovered at Cuzco and lent to the British Museum in London. One showed a blood group with an Rh factor that nobody had ever seen anywhere in this world before. Another mummy had a blood group that was very rare among other American Indians. Unfortunately, the experiments can not be repeated or expanded because all five mummies were destroyed when a water pipe burst in the basement of the British Museum. But it does look as if both the Egyptians and the Basques on one side of the Atlantic and the Incas on the other had blood that was different from that of the people living next to them. Was that the blood of the inhabitants of the sunken continent of Atlantis?

Another mystery is the similarity of customs on both sides of the Atlantic. Sumerians and Egyptians used the same art of mummification that was practiced by the Mayas and the Incas. They did this out of their belief in either a life after death or reincarnation and constructed pyramids to preserve and protect the departed. And now we have scientific proof that somehow the shape of the pyramid preserves, dessicates, and sterilizes organic matter, an effect that can be observed even in small pyramid-shaped containers made of plastic or cardboard. On both sides of the Atlantic pyramids were also constructed in ancient times as astronomical observatories, but that, probably, was not the primary reason for building them.

Above all, the similarity between all these cultures is demonstrated by the way they did their astronomical calculations and by the systems of measurement they developed. Obviously, they all observed the same stars and planets. Yet the fact that they made the calculations in exactly the same way and that from among so many other possible combinations in the movements of the celestial bodies they chose the very same conjunctions of the same planets is more than striking. It just could not have happened unless the Sumerians, the Egyptians, and Incas, the Aztecs, and the Mayas had either evolved from one central civilization, or were in constant contact with each other. And if there was a common center, it had to be a land in between the two sides of the Atlantic Ocean, the sunken continent of Atlantis.

Another equally striking similarity was the sun worship of the Egyptians and the Mayas, both of whom believed that their kings were sons of the sun god, even though the Egyptians, being more civilized, did not practice human sacrifice. Since the Egyptians did not colonize the Mayas or vice versa, the only logical explanation is that both cultures developed from a sun cult in a land of common origin, probably an island in the Atlantic.

Finally, on both sides of the Atlantic we find identical huge stone block edifices, built of cut pieces so heavy that even our present-day equipment cannot move them. If anybody doubts this, let him remember what happened only a few years ago, when an international task force helped save the gigantic Abu Simbel statues before completion of the Aswan High Dam in Egypt. The statues had to be cut into pieces for lifting and transportation.

On the west side of the Atlantic similar huge blocks were used at Cuzco and Tiahuanaco and also at the newly discovered underwater constructions near Bimini. On the east side we have the pyramids of Egypt and the gigantic stone slabs of Baalbek in Lebanon, a temple of totally unknown origin. The ruins of Baalbek, at an altitude of 3,800 feet, stand on a platform built of enormous stone blocks weighing more than 800 tons each. None of today's machines could move these megaliths or lift them. Such blocks must have been put in place either by giants or by beings of a civilization that knew the secrets of levitation and antigravity.

Three giant blocks from Baalbek now serve as the base of a Roman temple dedicated to Jupiter. The largest of these blocks measures 21 by 4 by 4 m, exactly: the two others are each 19.50 by 4 by 4 m. Together all three represent 60 m in length and 960 cu m in volume. These exact measurements make it nearly impossible to believe that the ancients who built Baalbek didn't know our metric system. Evidently they did not use our standard meter, but a cubit of 500 mm and a foot of 333 mm. For them, the length of 1 degree at the equator was equal to 222,222 cubits and their 1 minute of longitude measured 5,555 Baalbek ft.

For the constructors of this ancient site, the circumference of our globe was 80 million cubits, or 120 million ft, and this measurement unit of length seems to have common ground with the Sakkara foot, where metric dimensions were discovered and even a double meter standard found engraved on a wall.

The huge stones of Baalbek were cut out from bedrock 400 m away from the edifice and the quarry was set at a much lower level than the building site. It is there that another unfinished block was found, measuring 21.33 by 4.66 by 4.33 m; obviously, a block that would eventually have been cut to the exact size of 21 by 4 by 4 m, like the largest stone of the temple foundation. We will probably never know what caused the constructors of Baalbek to leave suddenly without finishing what they had begun, just as the statue carvers of Easter Island did, probably at the same time and for the same reason.

There is another group of stones that is probably related to the catastrophe of Atlantis. These are the megalithic monuments found only near the shores of the Atlantic in Europe and North Africa in the areas where people still speak the strange dialects, another confirmation of the theory that they all came from the same race of Atlantans, at one time spoke the same language, practiced the same sun cult, and constructed very similar megalithic monuments.

It appears now that as a group of refugees who survived the sinking of the continent and landed first on the West African coast, a majority of them moved north and reached first Morocco, then Spain, Portugal, France, and finally the British Isles.

Others went around Africa to Ceylon and the occidental part of India, where they constructed more than 2,000 megaliths. Some went farther on and reached Tibet, which explains how the authors of the Tibetan bible knew with such certainty the date of the great disaster of Atlantis and all the other precise details.

A very interesting book was published some time ago that registers the distribution of megalithic monuments all around the world and tells us that an enormous dolmen with a stone cover plate weighing 600 tons stands in eastern Korea, so it seems that refugees from the sunken Atlantis even got as far as that.

Until recently the general opinion was that the megalithic monuments of Europe were no more than about 3,000 years old, so nobody associated them with Atlantis that disappeared 12,000 years ago. But now when we have the first proofs that Atlantis really existed we also have discoveries indicating that some of the dolmens and menhirs are at least 10,000 years old or older. The young British archaeologist Colin Renfrew threw out all the old traditions and came up with a book proving that the megaliths of France, Spain, and Wales are much older than the tombs of Mycenae, the ziggurats of Mesopotamia, or even the pyramids of Egypt.

In other words, our civilization was not born in the Middle East, to be brought north into Europe. Just the opposite—it started in Western Europe and went down southeast toward Greece, Crete, Egypt, Mesopotamia, and western India.

Some who do not believe that Atlantis really existed might ask how come no artifacts have ever been found from the lost continent that could have been brought to Europe or the Mediterranean basin before the destruction of Atlantis. I have asked this question myself and I think that I have found an answer. No material except solid rock, which is not easily transported, and maybe solid gold, can last for 12,000 years. Most other materials oxidize and turn to dust. Besides, it is quite possible that some objects that fill our museums as unidentified primitive art and pagan idols are indeed remnants of Atlantis. The pure gold tablets in the museum in Cuenca are one example of such possibility. So were the many hieroglyph-covered gold statues and tablets that the Spanish conquistadors melted into ingots, destroying forever the great archaeological value that these relics possessed. Much of the evidence we now seek may have been destroyed centuries ago.

Luckily, however, there is one object, the only one that I know, that in my opinion comes from fabled Atlantis. It is unique at this moment and the only one of its kind in the whole world. It is the ceramic disk of Phaistos, thousands of years old, discovered by Sir Arthur Evans in the 1890s in the southern part of Crete under a thick layer of volcanic ashes. This ceramic disk, about 20 cm in diameter, is covered on both sides with hieroglyphs that nobody so far has been able to decipher.

The characters are displayed in a spiral form, starting in the center and turning counterclockwise. The signs are clustered in groups of one to seven, separated by a stroke. The virgules, as well as the spiral line that encloses the characters, are engraved. The signs themselves have been impressed in the soft clay by a stamp or a seal. Judging by the fine detail of these seals, they must have been made of metal and so immediately one is reminded of the mysterious gold tablet of Cuenca with its fifty-six hieroglyphs struck in the soft gold before it solidified, in order not to alter the standard weight.

Thirty of the undeciphered sign groups on the Phaistos disk are on one side, thirty-one on the other, which could suggest that it is a calendar based on alternating thirty- and thirty-one-day months, coming into phase every four years with the solar year. The cycle of such a calendar would be 1,461 days or twenty-seven months of thirty days each and twenty-one months of thirty-one days each. The hieroglyphs for each day could represent either the name of the day or what had to be done that day. Some scientists even think the disk may have been a navigational table. But so far nobody has been lucky enough to decipher and explain its use and significance. Neither can I, despite my conviction that this artifact stems from the fabled Atlantis and is proof of that continent's existence, as were the stone pavements found under water near Bimini.

The discovery near Bimini, in the Bahamas, incidentally, occurred just as predicted by the famous American seer Edgar Cayce, who in 1923 said that a temple of Atlantis would be found under water near Bimini in 1968. Even for someone who is

no admirer of occult sciences it is difficult to abstain from the belief that indeed Cayce must have had some contact with extraterrestrials who without any doubt must have known exactly
where the vestiges of Atlantis were to be found and who may
therefore some day give us *all* the information about the fabled
continent and its lost civilization.

CHAPTER 12

Contact with Extra-
terrestrial Civilizations

EARLY IN 1961, Otto Struve, the director of the National Science
Foundation's radio astronomy observatory at Green Bank, West
Virginia, and Frank Drake, his assistant, initiated Project Ozma
to search for radio signals from outer space, in order to determine if there were other civilizations in space trying to contact
us. Nobody was prepared for what was going to happen, even
those who had worked so long and so hard to finally get the authorization to perform the experiment.

There are several stars located at a reasonable distance from
the earth, only a few light-years away, suspected of having a
planetary system comparable to ours. For some reason, it was decided that the most favorable of these stars in 1961 was the star
Tau Ceti, a star in the constellation of Cetus, the Whale, which
is located close to the celestial equator and next to the constellation of Aries, the Ram.

The huge parabolic antenna of the observatory was aimed in
the direction of Tau Ceti; the mechanism of compensation for
the rotation of the earth was set in motion; then the receiver,
maser amplifier, and recorder were turned on. The only thing
left to be done was to wait, but those attending the experiment
did not have to wait too long.

Almost immediately, the needle of the recorder began indicating strong signals which, for any specialist in space com-

munications, could mean nothing but a coded message from an intelligent correspondent on a planet orbiting Tau Ceti. The signals lasted for about two minutes, then stopped, leaving those attending stupefied and unable to say a word. Finally, the whole thing was classified "secret" and that was the end of Project Ozma; it had lasted little more than two minutes.

However, there was a general feeling in the scientific circles of that time that a message from outer space had been received and deciphered but that, for some reason, it was decided that it could not be disclosed to the public. Since then a new Project Ozma has been initiated, but by military personnel this time.

The second case of communications with a space civilization, which was reported in *Paris-Match*, April 21, 1973, occurred in the Soviet Union. Two Russian specialists in space communications, Vsevolod Troitsky, director of the Radiophysics Research Institute of Gorki, and Nicolai Kardashev, director of the Space Research Institute in Moscow, were absolutely convinced that they had received radio signals from an extraterrestrial civilization.

They initiated their space listening program in 1970, with four radio frequency listening stations located far apart from each other. This allowed them, by comparing the received signals, to eliminate terrestrial interferences and keep only the space signals, those that were indentical from the four receiving stations. These signals from outer space whose duration varied from two to ten minutes, were repeated at regular intervals, following a regular pattern, which for these scientists indicated without any doubt that they had an artificial origin and that they were transmitted by intelligent beings whose culture was at least as advanced as ours.

The two Russian scientists have not succeeded so far in establishing the exact origin of these signals, but they are positive that they must originate from our solar system, either from another planet or from one of its satellites or even from an alien spacecraft from another solar system.

The third case of radio communications with outer space was that of the Izarian astronauts deciphered by Duncan Lunan and discussed in Chapter 1 of this book.

There is another case history which links extraterrestrial civilizations and flying saucers. Everyone knows the story of Barney and Betty Hill who disclosed under hypnosis that they had been kidnapped in a flying saucer in 1961, had undergone a physical examination, and had been shown a celestial map of the stars as seen from the planet of origin of the astronauts.

To tell you the truth, I did not believe a word of it at first. I only became interested in 1964 when Betty Hill was able, again under hypnosis, to reproduce the star map shown to her by the astronauts; but I was still skeptical about the whole thing. I thought maybe that time she was really going too far.

But then I really became fascinated when an amateur American astronomer named Marjorie Fish discovered that the celestial map shown to Betty Hill corresponded exactly to the one that could be seen from the star Zeta Reticuli, which is located in the southern hemisphere of the celestial vault, between the two bright stars Achernar and Canopus.

And I had good reasons to be excited because the main star drawn by Betty Hill on her map was a double star, and nobody on earth at that time, in 1961 or even in 1964, knew that Zeta Reticuli was a double star. This was only discovered in March 1973 by the American astronomer Peter Van de Camp, who specializes in that kind of research, especially the stars that move in spirals instead of straight lines, which indicates stars with a planetary system or double and triple stars.

Then I knew that Betty Hill had been telling the truth all the time, because there was no way she could have known that Zeta Reticuli was a double star when she was drawing the star map. Also, that map was drawn in a way that I have never seen anywhere on earth. The Reticulian astronauts, who were practical people rather than poets, linked their stars with traffic lines (double, single, or dotted), depending on the intensity of their traffic, instead of trying to draw bulls, lions, or even virgins as our ancestors used to do.

Over twenty years ago, an incredible phenomenon happened in France that is very little known (it was reported in the September 1959 issue of *Aerospace Engineering*, p. 46) but could very well have been a signal from an outer-space civilization for the purpose of informing us about their existence.

For almost five years, from 1953 to 1957, Maurice Allais, director of the French National Center of Scientific Research, performed in his underground laboratory of Saint Germain on the west side of Paris experiments in terrestrial gravitation with a 7,500-gr pendulum at the end of an 830-mm rod weighing 4,500 gr, or, in other words, a total pendulum weight of 12 kg.

As proven by the 1851 experiments of Léon Foucault, a pendulum always oscillates in the same plane with respect to outer space, in such a way that its plane of oscillation seems to rotate relatively to the surface of the earth.

The constant observation and recording of this apparent rotation and its variations, relative to the theoretical rotation that has been computed from astronomical data, allows a very accurate study of the different motions of the earth and, especially, of the regularity of its rotation around its polar axis.

On June 30, 1954, Maurice Allais was watching his pendulum with particular attention, for a total eclipse of the sun visible in Europe was to happen that day around noon, which eventually could slightly modify the plane of oscillation of the pendulum. But he certainly did not expect what did happen during that eclipse.

When the eclipse started, the plane of oscillation of the pendulum suddenly shifted by 15 degrees, from 170° to 185°. It stayed at 185° for the duration of the eclipse, but finally came back to its original position when the eclipse was over. As far as we know, this had never happened before and it has never happened since.

The announcement of this fantastic phenomenon made a lot of waves in scientific circles at the time and Allais was almost accused of having made up the whole story, but he was a very conscientious scientist and the angular shift of the pendulum was recorded by several of his instruments. It was indisputable. In the twenty years which have elapsed, numerous tentative explanations have been proposed without success.

Many scientists have been thinking for some time that outer space civilizations could very well have discovered a long time ago the secrets of gravitation, which they would thereafter know how to control and could use for the propulsion of their flying saucers. That would explain the incredible maneuvers UFOs perform in our skies, which have never been explained by the classical theories of official science.

Let us now suppose that they had decided some day to use gravitational forces to catch our attention and give us scientific proof of their existence. They would evidently have many different ways to do it, but one of the best would certainly be to use gravitational forces to disturb suddenly the observations made by our astronomers and physicists during a total eclipse of the sun, which would naturally be watched by thousands of scientists. Morever, that would have the additional advantage of being noticed only by scientists, without the risk of causing a panic in the general public.

Also, that phenomenon did not happen at the time of just any solar eclipse. It happened during one of those famous total solar eclipses that occur precisely on June 30 every nineteen years, like the last one on June 30, 1973, or the next one on June 30, 1992. Is it still really possible to believe that it was just another coincidence?

For that reason or some other, French scientists seem to take the problem of flying saucers very seriously. A few years ago a young French scientist by the name of Claude Poher, director of the French National Center of Space Research in Toulouse, decided to prove scientifically once and for all the actual existence of flying saucers and to establish their composite sketch, as reported in *Paris-Match*, March 23, 1974.

Out of 35,000 UFO observation reports that he had been able to collect, he selected the thousand best ones, translated them onto IBM punch cards, and fed them to a computer. Then he fed to the same computer the apparent characteristics of everything that could be seen in the sky and be mistaken for a flying saucer, like the planet Venus or weather balloons so dear to the U. S. Air Force, for the computer to compare with the UFO sightings and reach a final decision as to whether there was some correlation between the two kinds of data.

The verdict of the computer was that, first, flying saucers really do exist and cannot be confused with anything else in the sky. They have landed hundreds of times in deserted spots, far away from urban areas. They appear during the day as bright metallic objects reflecting sunlight and casting shadows, and during the night take on a yellowish or greenish-orange color. They can appear in the form of discs, spheres, or even cigars.

Seventy per cent of the observations were made at night, one in ten involved landings, and one in twenty were cases when extraterrestrial astronauts were seen by or had contacts with humans. Very powerful magnetic forces were always present in any case, and these forces could cut the power of automobile or aircraft generators, disturb radio transmissions, and make all kinds of on-board electromagnetic instruments go completely crazy.

Moreover, flying saucers can fly at more than 25,000 km an hour and suddenly fly back in the opposite direction, a maneuver that no space vehicle of human construction can do at present without disintegrating on the spot. Also, Poher has investigated eleven landing sites in France and found impressions on the ground similar to those that would have been left by a three-ski aircraft landing gear. The depth of these impressions indicates a weight of from 50 to 100 tons and a length of 200 to 300 m for the spacecraft. Also, nothing can now grow in those impressions, as if the ground had been burned.

I am not going to retell the story of Ezekiel and the flying saucer he saw near Babylon in 592 B.C. because you can read it in the Bible or in a very interesting book published a few years ago by one of my colleagues at NASA, *The Spaceships of Ezekiel* by Joseph Blumrich. But it is the oldest flying saucer report that I know of.

I think, however, that I should make a personal contribution. I think I know how flying saucers enter our solar system and, step by step, arrive near earth. In other words, I think that I have discovered their flight schedule.

In April 1973, when I was computing the revolution and conjunction periods of all the planets to verify the validity of the Nineveh number as a constant of the solar system, I was puzzled by the fact that Mars was in conjunction with the earth every 780 days, or every 2.135 years, while it was in conjunction with Jupiter every 816 days, or every 2.235 years, a difference of only 36 days.

Then I remembered reading a few months before that flying saucer invasions seemed to occur precisely every 800 days, or a little bit more than every two years. That was enough to put my

computer in motion and I discovered that the dates of flying saucer invasions corresponded precisely with the dates of Mars-
earth or Mars-Jupiter conjunctions.

Arriving from a faraway stellar system with a very high velocity, these spaceships could use the enormous gravitational attraction of the four big planets of our solar system to slow down and
settle into an orbit around Jupiter or one of its four largest satellites. There, like in an airport terminal, they could wait for
their connecting flight, the planet Mars, to pass by and then settle into an orbit around that planet. There they could wait again
for the earth to pass by and then settle into an orbit around the
earth or the moon.

In astronautic terms, passing from one planet to the next with
a minimum of fuel consumption is called "using a minimum energy orbit," and space astronauts might just do that. Anyway, for
the fun of it, and before we know for sure, I have established a
flight schedule for outer space travelers arriving on earth and,
believe it or not, it checks perfectly with the dates of the latest
flying saucer invasions.

Of course, the interval between two flights will never be exactly 780 or 816 days, because of elliptical orbits, but do you
know one single airline that is always on time? Anyway, for op-
timal precision in arrival time the Mars-Jupiter and Mars-earth
flights will coincide every 143 years, the next time being in 1980.

Conclusion

Years ago, when I decided to write this book, I wanted to try to prove the accuracy of three of my favorite theories that would help explain many great mysteries of the past. Long before I tried to present my ideas, many other men had made their attempts to explain the same phenomena, but they did not quite succeed, I think, because they started from the wrong premises.

The first of my theories states that even tens of thousands of years ago our ancestors possessed amazingly precise scientific knowledge, especially in astronomy and mathematics. But if we accept the official scientific views of today, such advanced knowledge was quite impossible, because at that time man barely knew how to make a crude flint axe and had not even invented the wheel.

My second theory states that this astounding knowledge was given to mankind by extraterrestrial voyagers—astronauts who came from outer space, with a much higher civilization and culture. It states that, little by little, these astronauts created modern man by insemination and mutation. Our primitive ancestors were thus quickly transformed from Neanderthal men into Cro-Magnon men, the strong and intelligent beings that appeared on earth about 65,000 years ago.

My third theory states that this unbelievably high scientific knowledge of our ancestors, as well as their religious beliefs and their social customs, identical in all four corners of the earth, had to come from one common source that in relatively recent times seemed to have been situated somewhere in the middle of the Atlantic Ocean, but in a more distant past was located in the Pacific.

These centers disappeared without a trace in cosmic cataclysms, leaving only distant memories, inherited from a few survivors, which were reflected in ceremonies, sagas, and some sacred texts.

I have tried to prove the accuracy of these theories by using numbers, even though I know that many people dislike numbers and figures. To these readers I offer my apologies, but I had no choice. For the benefit of those who may still doubt the accuracy of the evidence presented in the preceding chapters of this book, I will summarize my facts.

The scientific knowledge of astronomy shown by our ancestors tens of thousands of years ago was far superior to that of astronomers only 300 years ago.

Our prehistoric ancestors knew that the celestial dome is fixed and that the sun, the moon, and the planets rotate. They had noticed that the triangle formed by the stars Sirius, Procyon, and Betelgeuse is immovably fixed, while other constellations, like the Great Bear, change their relative positions imperceptibly over many thousands of years. That was why the ancient astronomers chose the star Sirius as the base for their long-range calculations.

They knew without doubt that the earth revolves around the sun and that the moon revolves around the earth. They knew about the existence of the planets Uranus and Neptune even though it is very rarely possible to see Uranus with the naked eye and impossible to see Neptune at all. They also knew that Mars has two satellites, Jupiter four, Saturn seven, and Uranus two. They knew that comets reappeared at fixed intervals. Some astronomers of the past even knew about the existence of the planet Pluto, which we "discovered" only very recently, and these astronomers of mankind's early dawn even suspected the existence of another planet beyond Pluto, which they named Proserpine. We still have not found this distant planet, but many present-day astronomers are quite sure that it does exist . . .

The ancient astronomers also knew that the two points where the equator intersects the earth's solar orbit during equinoxes shift in a westerly direction by 1 degree every 72 years, or by 360 degrees in 25,920 years.

This phenomenon that for thousands of years was known in many parts of the earth was forgotten for a long time, and the Christian Church ignored it until only three hundred years ago.

Our ancestors also knew that the period of 25,920 years was the time elapsed for one rotation of the terrestrial axis at 23½° around the celestial axis, and they called this period of time the "Great Year." And they knew that this rotation explained why the polar star was not always the same and why other circumpolar stars were sometimes visible and sometimes not.

Finally, our ancestors knew that all the planets and satellites in our solar system return to the same position on the celestial vault after 2,268 million days, or after 6.3 million years of 360 days each, a timespan that for modern astronomy equals 6,209,578 years of 365.2422 days each.

In mathematics instead of the decimal system, our ancestors used fractions which were much more precise than our decimals. They did not use the decimal system because they did not have a need for it—they did not have decimal calculators. The use of fractions instead of approximated decimal values gave them a system that allowed them to resolve, for instance, the squaring of the circle. The squaring of the circle is the computation of a square with exactly the same perimeter as a given circle. This is considered impossible by our modern mathematicians, who use the value of π as a number of infinite decimals. For our ancestors, π was the ratio 22:7. Therefore, a circle with a radius of 7 had a perimeter of 44, the same as a square with a side of 11.

The Golden Section (or factor ϕ), which allows us to construct triangles or rectangles having the same surface area as a given circle, was expressed by the ratio 196:121. The square root of this number used by our ancient ancestors was 14:11, which equals 4:π, or 28:22. Consequently, a circle with a radius of 14:11 has a surface of 56:11, the same square area as a rectangle with sides of 22:7 and 196:121, or a triangle with a base of 44:7 and a height of 196:121.

Angles too were expressed as fractions. These could, depending on the case, represent the functions of sine, cosine, or tangent of the angles. So, sine of 30° was ½, cosine of 60° was equal to 13/15, and the tangent of the base angle of the Great Pyramid was 14/11, the square root of the Golden Section.

The angle of inclination of the earth's rotational axis with the action of the ecliptic was defined by its cosine value, or the fraction 11/12, found in the dimensions of the Kalasasaya Temple in Tiahuanaco, which measures 264×288 cubits, and in those of many other temples around the world.

But this temple in Tiahuanaco was probably constructed 27,000 years ago, as can be seen by its astronomical layout, and, if nothing else testifies about its age, it is the condition of the ruins which prove to us that much more than 10,000 years have elapsed since it was built. It is therefore evident that our ancestors of 10,000 or more years ago possessed a level of mathematical and astronomical knowledge so superior that they could not have developed it by themselves.

With this conclusion, we arrive at my second theory, namely, the intervention of some extraterrestrial source in human affairs many thousands of years ago. This theory is already generally accepted by the public and also is considered a possibility by part of the scientific community, but it is difficult to get the official scientific establishment to accept this theory because it would turn upside down all traditional scientific beliefs. Nevertheless, this theory is true and accurate, because there is none other that would better explain the sudden appearance of intelligent man and his very advanced scientific knowledge so long ago. Also, there are many proofs of ancient technical knowledge that could only have reached our ancestors by direct transmission from a more highly developed culture. Let me cite a few examples:

Our ancient ancestors knew and used static electricity, electric current, wetcell batteries, electroplating, and powerful light projectors fed by high-voltage cables. They used platinum, a metal that melts only at 1,753° C, and aluminum, which allegedly wasn't discovered and produced until the nineteenth century.

Our ancestors knew optics. Possibly they even used telescopes and microscopes, because perfectly polished optical lenses, made out of glass or quartz, have been found in various archaeological sites.

It is also very likely that they knew the secret of gravitation and used it to perform levitation—something we cannot even explain today. Without this knowledge of gravitational control, our ancestors could not have built edifices of enormous stone slabs, which have been found all over the world. No modern construction cranes could lift the huge stones of the temple at Baalbek, once the ancient town of Heliopolis, northeast of Beirut, Lebanon.

In several places on the globe somebody traced gigantic figures and geometric designs like those in Nasca, the Maltese cross in the Aegean Sea, or the Triangle of France. None of these figures and designs could have been created by humans standing on the ground. Flying machines and possibly electromagnetic navigation devices were needed to trace these huge markers, which could be seen and recognized only from high up in the sky. Humans of that period did not have the technology needed to fly nor the necessary electromagnetic distance-measuring equipment. It seems that the only valid explanation is that these machines were built somewhere else in space and brought here by astronauts to improve and to educate the human race.

My third theory, which states that all terrestrial civilizations evolved from the same source, is probably the easiest to prove. With the exception of some references in ancient legends, there are no remaining traces of the mysterious Land of Mu, the continent that existed perhaps only 100,000 years ago in the middle of the Pacific Ocean and that certainly will be found someday on the ocean floor. But many clues exist today which prove the existence of Atlantis and its culture that linked east with west, the Eurasian continent with the Americas, until it too disappeared some 12,000 years ago.

We have found some of the ruins of Atlantis underwater in the Bahamas. Also, there is no better explanation than the common source of Atlantis to make us understand the astounding similarities between ancient civilizations on both sides of the Atlantic Ocean, like the Mayan and Egyptian, both of which had pyramids, mummies, close intermarriage, the same basic measurement and calculation techniques, and many other things in common. A large number of serious people do not doubt that Atlantis existed. What is still left for us to find out is its exact placement on the map and the exact amount of time that elapsed between the creation and disappearance of the famed sunken continent.

As one could see from this book, I did succeed in solving some of the problems that were posed to me during my visit at the astronautical congress in Paris some years ago. Since my specialty was space communications, it seemed logical for me to start by trying to solve the mysteries of UFOs and extraterrestrial civilizations. But I am also a mathematician, and I had a vague feeling that at least some of these problems could be resolved by using numbers and electronic calculators. It seems that these assumptions were correct. One single number—the constant of the solar system—solved more than one of my mysteries and only the first three problems were really difficult to decipher. The rest were resolved in a relatively much simpler way because I used the method of efficient calculating. I started with the mysterious number of fifteen digits found in Nineveh and soon discovered that it was the esoteric form, expressed in seconds, of the much simpler number of 2,268 million days, or just about 6.3 million years. When I discovered later that this time span represented exactly 240 equinoctial cycles, which always played a prominent role in ancient astrology, I immediately realized that by sheer luck I had found the Great Constant of the Solar System, lost for many centuries, and it happened without my even looking for it.

My discovery that this Solar, or Nineveh, Constant had been calculated 64,800 years ago, at the time when Cro-Magnon man suddenly appeared on the earth, made me feel that I had hit the jackpot.

Up to now, none of our classic theories could satisfactorily explain the sudden appearance of the Cro-Magnon man on earth. And no one using the classic theories of evolution will ever explain how the Cro-Magnon, immediately upon arrival, could calculate the Nineveh Constant based on the planets Uranus and Neptune, which he couldn't even see, and the imperceptible displacement of the equinoctial point that shifts west by only 1 degree every 72 years.

In my opinion, both these mysteries have just one explanation

—the intervention of astronauts from another world, who came, just as the Bible tells us, to create, educate, and civilize a new human race in their own image.

Thus, once upon a time, about 65,000 years ago, extraordinary visitors came from another civilization in space, discovered the earth was a wonderful place to live on, and decided to establish a colony here. But in the beginning they did not like our air and water, and they weren't used to the earth's gravity. So, these visitors decided to create a hybrid race, so that by crossbreeding with humans after a few generations, that new race would be perfectly adapted to life on earth and would carry on at least part of the intelligence and technical know-how of its ancestors from space. To achieve this, the most attractive and the most intelligent young females were inseminated, and this procedure continued with their daughters and granddaughters until the results were acceptable for life on earth, and the education and civilization of the new race could start.

Another mystery I tried to solve was that of the Mayan calendar. Once I knew the Nineveh Constant and the exact periods of revolution and conjunction of planets, it didn't take long to find the only astronomical period that had a duration of about 20 years. I had more trouble with the starting date of the Mayan calendar, but I knew that it too had to be a date of conjunction between two planets other than Jupiter and Saturn. So I tried Uranus and Neptune and discovered the cycle of a quadruple conjunction of 4,627 years that is hardly known. After that came the realization that the Mayas, who were obsessed with calculations using enormous numbers, used the number 34,020 million days—a number fifteen times greater than the Nineveh Constant —and that this number corresponded exactly to 3,600 Sumerian cycles of precession of the equinoxes.

Then we had the mystery of the Great Pyramid of Cheops, which was based on three different mathematical principles, incompatible if expressed in decimals, but compatible when expressed as fractions. The pyramid was at the same time an astronomical observatory, a standard of weights and measures, and a standard of time. Both its volume and the length of the coffer in its royal chamber were based on the Solar Constant.

The Maltese cross, the Rhodes calculator, and the navigational systems of the ancient seafarers did not give me much trouble. I found the solutions by accident while trying to solve other problems. As for the signs of the zodiac, the polar rounds, and the universal calendar, I was greatly helped by the research work done by others before me. I have listed their publications in the bibliography at the end of this book.

The last three puzzles—those of the four moons, of Atlantis, and of the extraterrestrial visitors—really fascinated me, because they were at the outer limits between science and complete mystery, and I needed more than numbers and computers to solve them. I needed intuition, just as I needed intuition in discovering the Nineveh Constant, the secrets of the Mayan calendar, and the mystery of the Great Pyramid of Cheops. I am convinced that to resolve all this in a few weeks' time would not have been possible without the help of some occult power source that is unknown to me now and will probably remain unknown to me forever.

I have been helped in my research just as our ancestors were aided tens of thousands of years ago. Can anyone really think that all the fantastic knowledge in astronomy, mathematics, geodesy, and many other sciences was acquired by mankind without outside help? Frankly, is it not much more logical to accept the idea that all this knowledge was brought by astronauts who came from another world, just as many legends and the Bible tell us, or that the advancement of mankind was stimulated by some very highly developed cultures located in the Land of Mu or Atlantis, which were visited even earlier by outside civilizations from within the solar system or even from distant galaxies?

As recently as twenty years ago it was permissible to question and dismiss such theories as incredible. But in the last two decades we ourselves walked on the moon and drove a jeep on its surface, and our space probes have flown at low altitudes over Venus, Mars, and Mercury and have taken magnificent photographs of the latter two planets. We have a space probe under way that will make a tour of the solar system beyond Saturn. And the possibility and hypothesis that our ancestors were visited from space by extraterrestrial beings does no longer seem so impossible. Indeed, such thoughts began to seem very logical.

A few more years and a few more space explorations from now, our children will ask in wonderment why such theories seemed so implausible to previous generations.

It is evident that all the theories and hypotheses that I have formulated here are subject to further verification, and it is possible that some will be proven inexact, as is often the case in this kind of exploration, touching on the outer limits of exact sciences. But that seems to be of lesser importance to me, at least as far as we are concerned now.

What is important is to launch and set in motion new ideas, so that these can inspire subsequent generations to make their own discoveries and formulate new theories.

In the past, most men who came up with new thoughts and concepts were dismissed as fools, provided they were lucky enough not to be burned alive, as the Roman Catholic Church did to Giordano Bruno in the year 1600, because he was so naïve as to believe that the universe was infinite and that many other worlds similar to ours existed, where the inhabitants could live in peace because the Inquisition didn't exist there.

In our times the honest search for truth is less likely to lead to violent death, but the risk still exists. There are quite a few American UFO researchers who have complained about death threats received either by phone or by mysterious visitors demanding that they cease their activities. Some have actually died under strange circumstances and all their collected materials have disappeared without a trace. That could explain why we will never know the complete truth about all the riddles of the universe.

Bibliography

BAILEY, JAMES. *The God Kings and the Titans.* St. Martin's, New York, 1973.

BAKER, ROBERT, and LAURENCE FREDRICK. *Introduction to Astronomy.* Van Nostrand, New York, 1968.

BARRAU, JACQUES, ed. *Plants and Migrations of Pacific Peoples.* Bishop Museum, Honolulu, 1963.

BARRY, GEORGES. *Les Nombres Magiques Nucléaires.* Dervy, Paris, 1975.

BELLAMY, HANS, and PETER ALLEN. *The Calendar of Tiahuanaco.* Faber & Faber, London, 1956.

BERGIER, JACQUES. *Extraterrestrial Visitations.* Regnery, Chicago, 1973.

BIBBY, GEOFFREY. *Looking for Dilmun.* Knopf, New York, 1970.

BIRAUD, FRANÇOIS, and JEAN RIBES. *Civilisations extraterrestres.* Fayard, Paris, 1970.

BIRNEY, D. SCOTT. *Modern Astronomy.* 2d ed. Allyn & Bacon, Boston, 1974.

BLEEKER, SONIA. *The Maya.* Morrow, New York, 1961.

BLUMRICH, JOSEPH. *The Spaceships of Ezekiel.* Bantam, New York, 1974.

BRAINERD, GEORGE. *The Maya Civilization.* Southwest Museum, Los Angeles, 1968.

BRONOWSKI, JACOB. *The Ascent of Man.* Little, Brown, Boston, 1973.

BROWN, RAYMOND. *Phantoms of the Sea.* Taplinger, New York, 1973.

BUSHNELL, GEORGE. *The First Americans.* McGraw-Hill, New York, 1968.

CARNAC, PIERRE. *Les Conquérants du Pacifique.* Laffont, Paris, 1975.

CERAM, C.W. *Gods, Graves, and Scholars.* Knopf, New York, 1951.

CHARPENTIER, LOUIS. *Mysteries of Chartres Cathedral.* Avon, New York, 1975.

CHARROUX, ROBERT. *Forgotten Worlds.* Walker, New York, 1973.

CHUBB, MARY. *City in the Sand.* Crowell, New York, 1957.

COTTRELL, LEONARD. *Lost Cities.* Holt, Rinehart & Winston, New York, 1957.

COUSTEAU, JACQUES, and PHILIPPE DIOLÉ. *Diving for Sunken Treasure.* Doubleday, Garden City, N.Y., 1972.

DANIEL, GLYN. *The Megalith Builders.* Penguin, Harmondsworth, England, 1968.

DÄNIKEN, ERICH VON. *The Gold of the Gods.* Trans. M. Heron. Putnam, New York, 1973.

DAVIDSON, BASIL. *Lost Cities of Africa.* Little, Brown, Boston, 1959.

DAVIES, NIGEL. *The Aztecs.* Putnam, New York, 1973.

DE SANTILLANA, GIORGIO, and HERTHA VON DECHEND. *Hamlet's Mill.* Gambit, Boston, 1969.

DOWNING, BARRY. *The Bible and Flying Saucers.* Avon, New York, 1970.

DRAKE, RAYMOND. *Gods and Spacemen of the Ancient West.* Signet, New York, 1974.

FLEMMING, NICHOLAS. *Cities in the Sea.* Doubleday, Garden City, N.Y., 1971.

FLINDT, MAX, and OTTO BINDER. *Mankind Child of the Stars.* Fawcett World, Greenwich, Conn., 1974.

GALLANT, ROY A. *Astrology: Sense or Nonsense.* Doubleday, Garden City, N.Y., 1974.

GAUQUELIN, MICHEL. *Les Horloges Cosmiques.* Denoel, Paris, 1970.

GIDDINGS, LOUIS. *Ancient Men of the Arctic.* Knopf, New York, 1967.

GRANGER, MICHEL. *Extraterrestres en exil.* Michel, Paris, 1975.

GUERRIER, ERIC. *La Cosmogonie des Dogons.* Laffont, Paris, 1975.

GUINGAMP, MAURICE. *Notre Dame de Paris.* Laffont, Paris, 1972.

HAPGOOD, CHARLES. *The Path of the Poles.* Chilton, Philadelphia, 1970.

HAWKINS, GERALD. *Beyond Stonehenge.* Harper & Row, New York, 1973.

HAWKES, JACQUETTA. *Prehistoric Britain.* Penguin, Harmondsworth, England, 1944.

HENNIG, RICHARD. *Les Grandes Énigmes de l'univers.* Laffont, Paris, 1957.

HUTIN, SERGE. *History of Astrology.* Pyramid, New York, 1972.

HYNEK, ALLEN. *The UFO Experience.* Regnery, Chicago, 1972.

IRWIN, CONSTANCE. *Fair Gods and Stone Faces.* St. Martin's, New York, 1963.

JESSUP, RONALD. *The Wonderful World of Astrology.* Doubleday, Garden City, N.Y., 1968.

KELLER, WERNER. *The Bible as History.* Bantam, New York, 1974.

KEYHOE, DONALD. *Flying Saucers, Top Secret.* Putnam, New York, 1960.

KOLOSIMO, PETER. *Timeless Earth.* Bantam, New York, 1975.

KUBNICK, HENRI. *La Grande Peur de l'an 2000.* Michel, Paris, 1974.

LANDSBURG, ALAN. *In Search of Ancient Mysteries.* Bantam, New York, 1974.

LE POER TRENCH, BRINSLEY. *Mysterious Visitors: The UFO Story.* Stein & Day, New York, 1973.

LEY, WILLY. *Another Look at Atlantis.* Doubleday, Garden City, N.Y., 1969.

LISSNER, IVAR. *Civilisations mystérieuses.* Laffont, Paris, 1964.

LUNAN, DUNCAN. *Man and the Stars.* Souvenir Press, London, 1974.

MACGOWAN, KENNETH. *Early Man in the New World.* Macmillan, New York, 1950.

MACNEICE, LOUIS. *Astrology.* Doubleday, Garden City, N.Y., 1964.

MARSHACK, ALEXANDER. *The Roots of Civilization.* McGraw-Hill, New York, 1971.

MAZEL, JEAN. *Avec les Phéniciens.* Laffont, Paris, 1968.

MAZIÈRE, FRANCIS. *Expedition Tumuc-Humac.* Trans. F. G. Renier and A. Cliff. Doubleday, New York, 1955.

MERTZ, HENRIETTE. *Gods from the Far East: How the Chinese Discovered America.* Ballantine, New York, 1975.

MICHEL, HENRI. *Scientific Instruments in History.* Viking, New York, 1967.

MISRAKI, PAUL. *Des Signes dans le ciel.* Labergerie, Paris, 1968.

MITCHELL, SAMUEL A. *Eclipses of the Sun.* Columbia University Press, New York, 1923.

MOONEY, RICHARD. *Colony Earth.* Fawcett, New York, 1975.

MOREAU, MARCEL. *Civilisations des étoiles.* Laffont, Paris, 1973.
MORGAN, ELAINE. *The Descent of Woman.* Stein & Day, New York, 1972.
NAGLE, JAMES. *Heredity and Human Affairs.* Mosby, St. Louis, 1974.
NEUBERT, OTTO. *La Vallée des rois.* Laffont, Paris, 1954.
NIEL, FERNAND. *The Mysteries of Stonehenge.* Avon, New York, 1975.
PAUWELLS, LOUIS, and JACQUES BERGIER. *The Morning of the Magicians.* Avon, New York, 1968.
PEARSON, KENNETH. *The Dorak Affair.* Atheneum, New York, 1968.
PINNEY, ROY. *Underwater Archaeology.* Hawthorne, New York, 1970.
POCHAN, ANDRÉ. *L'Énigme de la grande pyramide.* Laffont, Paris, 1971.
POESSON, PAUL. *Le Testament de Noé.* Laffont, Paris, 1972.
RACKL, HANS. *Diving into the Past.* Scribner, New York, 1968.
RENFREW, COLIN. *Before Civilization.* Knopf, New York, 1973.
SAGAN, CARL. *The Cosmic Connection.* Doubleday, Garden City, N.Y., 1973.
SANDERSON, IVAN. *Invisible Residents.* World, New York, 1970.
SAURAT, DENIS. *Atlantis and the Giants.* Faber & Faber, London, 1957.
SCHWARTZ, JEON-MICHAEL. *Mysteries of Easter Island.* Avon, New York, 1975.
SENDY, JEAN. *The Coming of the Gods.* Berkley, New York, 1973.
SILVERBERG, ROBERT. *Before the Sphinx.* Nelson, New York, 1971.
SOLECKI, RALPH. *Shanidar: The First Flower People.* Knopf, New York, 1971.
SOUSTELLE, JACQUES. *Daily Life of the Aztecs on the Eve of the Spanish Conquest.* Stanford Univ. Press, 1961.
STAHLMAN, WILLIAM, and OWEN GINGERICH. *Solar and Planetary Longitudes.* University of Wisconsin Press, Madison, 1963.
STEINHAUSER, GÉRARD. *Les Chrononautes.* Michel, Paris, 1973.
SUGGS, ROBERT. *Modern Discoveries in Archaeology.* Crowell, New York, 1962.
TARADE, GUY. *Les Dossiers de l'étrange.* Laffont, Paris, 1971.
THOMPSON, ERIC. *The Dresden Codex.* American Philosophical Society, Philadelphia, 1972.
THROCKMORTON, PETER. *The Lost Ships.* Little, Brown, Boston, 1969.
TOMAS, ANDREW. *We Are Not the First.* Bantam, New York, 1971.
TOMPKINS, PETER. *The Secrets of the Great Pyramid.* Harper & Row, New York, 1971.
UMLAND, ERIC, and CRAIG UMLAND. *Mystery of the Ancients: Early Spacemen and the Mayas.* Signet, New York, 1975.
VALLEE, JACQUES. *Passport to Magonia: From Folklore to Flying Saucers.* Regnery, Chicago, 1969.
VAUGHAN, AGNES. *House of the Double Axe: The Palace at Knossos.* Doubleday, Garden City, N.Y., 1959.
VELIKOVSKY, IMMANUEL. *Worlds in Collision.* Doubleday, Garden City, N.Y., 1950.
VIEUX, MAURICE. *Les Secrets des batisseurs.* Laffont, Paris, 1975.
VON HAGEN, VICTOR. *Ancient Sun Kingdoms.* World, New York, 1957.
WAISBARD, SIMONE. *Tiahuanaco.* Laffont, Paris, 1971.
WOOLEY, LEONARD. *Ur of the Chaldees.* Penguin, Harmondsworth, England, 1954.